Praise for

Through The Fire - A Woman's Guide To Transformation

"Each woman makes a commitment to personal growth in her own way. *Through The Fire: A Woman's Guide To Transformation* provides a map for those willing to truly look within. An extraordinary and sometimes humorous guide, Winkelman has used her own life and her own art to create psychological signposts along the way. Regardless of what stage of life the reader is in, this book will encourage her to delve more deeply into herself."
>Diana Daffner, M.A., Counselor
>Workshop Leader and Author of *Tantric Sex for Busy Couples*

"*Through the Fire* is a journey of complete awakening and insight into feminine transformation ...a beautiful showcase of personal artwork and a real pleasure to read. It will assist any woman in her spiritual evolution, as well as dealing with life's conflicts at any stage of life. The self-help portion is a gift to women who want to keep track of their own development."
>Dr. Light Miller
>Author and Educator of Ayurvedic Medicine

"*Through The Fire: A Woman's Guide To Transformation* is an amazing storytelling of the extra-ordinary stages all women encounter on their journey of life. It left me feeling uplifted, understood, and encouraged to explore the next stage of my growth! I highly recommend Satya's understandable work for any woman who is exploring personal growth."
>Dr. Jenny White
>Artist and Educator

"*Through The Fire*, with Satya's artwork, is amazing and I can see myself in all of those stages. Thank you for opening the door of change for me and for the difference this will make for all women."
>Cherie DiNoia, CFP
>Personal Growth Seminar Leader and Registered Investment Advisor

"I could relate to all of the sculptures and the stages of evolution in *Through The Fire* as it tells all of our stories. I loved it."
>Susan Weston McMillian, M.S., Licensed Mental Health Counselor
>Director of Affordable Counseling and the Domestic Abuse Intervention Project

Through The Fire

Through The Fire

A Woman's Guide to Transformation

Satya Winkelman, M.A.

with

Ginger Merrill Perlman

Take-Action Press, LLC

Sarasota, Florida

Copyright © 2008 by Satya Winkelman

All rights reserved. No part of this publication may be reproduced or transmitted in any form or by any means electronic or mechanical, including photocopy, recording, or any information storage and retrieval system now known or to be invented, without permission in writing from the publisher, except by a reviewer who wishes to quote brief passages in connection with a review written for inclusion in a magazine, newspaper, or broadcast.

Design by George Cieszka

ISBN 978-0-9824559-0-6

Published in the United States by
Take-Action Press, LLC
PO Box 19174
Sarasota, Florida 34276

This book is dedicated to the memory of my mother, Ruth, who was a model of courage, strength, and perseverance. When life got painful and difficult, she would remind me "This too will change." And it did.

Acknowledgments

Thanks to the hundreds of women who have trusted me with their stories, journeys and hearts and whose struggles and striving for growth have been a constant inspiration to me.

I'd like to acknowledge and thank artists Janice Bowers and Juliana Montane, who contributed their talented photographic skills, and to Sami Blouin's keen editorial eye.

Also, my appreciation to Ginger Merrill Perlman, who played an important role in helping me to create this book. While being a joy to work with, she organized my writings and lectures, shared her impressions of my art and helped put my ideas and concepts into words.

Special thanks to my dear friend and sweetheart, George Cieszka, who has given his computer skills, love and support, and to my sons, Michael and Josh, who have participated in my growth more than they know.

Last but not least, to all of my teachers, especially Yogi Amrit Desai, who taught me the meaning of acceptance.

Contents

Prologue 15
Introduction 21

STAGE ONE : MAIDENING - PREPARING

Chapter 1: The Age of Formation 25
Chapter 2: The Age of Attraction 31

STAGE TWO : MOTHERING - PRODUCING

Chapter 3: The Age of Attachment 47
Chapter 4: The Age of Selflessness 51

STAGE THREE : MORPHING - FIRING

Chapter 5: The Age of Discontent 63
Chapter 6: The Age of Cocooning 71

STAGE FOUR : MATURING - FINISHING

Chapter 7: The Age of Breakthrough 87
Chapter 8: The Age of Truth 93

STAGE FIVE : MATRONING - FREEING

Chapter 9: The Age of Acceptance 107
Chapter 10: The Age of Wisdom 113
Chapter 11: The Age of Completion 121

Illustrations

Figure	1	In the Beginning	26
Figure	2	Egg Girl	27
Figure	3	Opening	28
Figure	4	Pretty Butt Naïve	32
Figure	5	I Can Do It Anyway	33
Figure	6	Cocksure	35
Figure	7	Waiting for the Groom	37
Figure	8	Anything to Please	48
Figure	9	Holding Time	49
Figure	10	Our Lady of Perpetual Giving	52
Figure	11	Hanging On	53
Figure	12	Bewilderment	64
Figure	13	Turning Away	66
Figure	14	More Than Annoyed	67
Figure	15	Stop!	69
Figure	16	Our Lady of Sorrow	73
Figure	17	Cloak of the Unknown	74
Figure	18	Wrapped Up in Myself	76
Figure	19	Letting Go	88
Figure	20	The Light is Within	89
Figure	21	Mothering Herself	90
Figure	22	Head in Her Heart	94
Figure	23	Centurion of Consciousness	96
Figure	24	Mind-Body	98
Figure	25	No Body's Perfect	108

Illustrations

Figure 26	Decorate Herself	110
Figure 27	Courage	111
Figure 28	Feminine Landscape	114
Figure 29	Kneeling Crone	115
Figure 30	Standing Meditation	117
Figure 31	Sitting Meditation	117
Figure 32	Retiring	119
Figure 33	Completion	122
Figure 34	It's All Clay	123
Figure 35	It's All Clay - Spirit Woman	124

Prologue

Satya's Thoughts

This book came into being because of a surprising image that appeared in a photo of my artwork. Although I have been facilitating personal growth and empowerment seminars for thirty years, I've been a very private person and have kept my art for myself. I've used the process of creating sensuous clay goddesses as a personal expression for my own psyche and soul. Then it happened. I was shown a photo of the sculpted empty black bowl, "It's All Clay". There, to my amazement, looking straight at the woman on the edge of the bowl was a face that appeared from the camera's flash of light. For years, I resisted writing about the concepts I had developed and taught. However, after the initial shock of seeing that figure, I interpreted the image to mean Spirit was directing me to go through my resistance and share my work.

Image in bowl - "It's All Clay"

After viewing all the photos, which now appear in this book, I realized there was an order to them. They clearly illustrated the five stages of feminine development that I have been teaching and personally experiencing. I had been subconsciously creating these stages in clay.

Bowl - "It's All Clay"

At first, I just used these photos in Woman's Retreats I conducted. They helped the women understand where they were in this transformative process of becoming more conscious, more aware and truly authentic. Then, in my private practice, clients kept asking to see them. When I organized the photos into an album, they could relate directly to the images without going into their own stories. Just by seeing the sequence of photographs, they became relieved that they were not alone or stuck! They could tell where they were, where they had been, and where they were headed on their own journey of authenticity just by looking.

The next step happened at a Wise Woman Workshop I was leading. Ginger Perlman, a talented writer in the group, expressed eagerness to help put my teachings into book form as well.

It has been a passion of mine to help awaken women to their full potential and throughout my entire psychotherapy career, I have been encouraging them to do so. However, it seems more important now than ever before! We no longer can look outside ourselves for authorities to heal our ills. Each of us must look within to discover our own feminine voice of nurturing, compassion and emotional expression.

Ultimately, each one of us must balance the masculine and feminine energies within before we can expect to see balance without. Although this book is directed to women, as my art and experience have been from a woman's perspective, men might also benefit by strengthening their awareness and expression of the feminine principle. It is from this balance we can heal and experience harmony.

The journey of transformation to a higher consciousness is not an easy one. I invite you to join with me in self-examination and expression to create and manifest your inner truths and birth your Wise Woman *Though The Fire* of transformation.

Enjoy the journey...

Namaste, Satya Winkelman

Ginger's Thoughts

When Satya first came into my life, I was lost in my "snow globe" phase. As a young girl, snow globes had been one of my favorite Christmas stocking surprises – those idyllic winter wonderlands captured within the confines of their small plastic domes. I felt such power knowing that with one twist of my tiny wrist, this miniature village could be turned upside down – its calm peacefulness upended by the chaos of a swirling blizzard.

This is exactly the way my own world felt at that time – topsy-turvy and out of control. I had left the security of a 27-year marriage in search of a life with more meaning, passion and purpose. Little did I know that what I really was searching for was my true Authentic Self.

Feeling like a stranger masquerading as me, I had one foot grounded in my familiar past and the other reaching out for the slippery edge of my future. My mind and heart were caught somewhere in between the two in a disconcerting limbo-land. It was impossible for me to see the path that lay ahead, blinded as I was by an internal blizzard of self-doubt, uncertainty, blame and shame.

Then everything changed…

According to the principle of attraction, we draw exactly what we need to ourselves, when we are ready and open to receiving it. That is when Satya and her teachings entered my life. In the course of one life-altering weekend workshop, I was able to find my footing once again and start moving forward with renewed hope and clarity. With Satya's art serving as tools for self-discovery, I saw myself reflected in her sculpture "Bewilderment" and realized that I had entered the Age of Discontent. Under Satya's guidance, I came to understand that this was a painful but necessary phase I must walk through on the road to higher consciousness. Knowing that more rewarding days lay ahead inspired me to take the difficult steps needed to get to the next chapter of my life.

Bewilderment

To my delight, I learned that the principle of attraction could work both ways. Satya recognized in me, the writer/editor she had been searching for to get her teachings "out there" as a book.

The experience of working with this multi-talented artist, teacher and Wise Woman has been a creative dream fulfilled for me and has opened the gateway to my own personal growth and healing. With the completion of each page, I could feel myself growing and changing– challenging my outmoded old beliefs, releasing negative behaviors that no longer served me and evolving into an increasingly Wise Woman myself.

Today I am living proof of the transformative possibility found in the words and wisdom of this book and believe it is a must-read for every woman searching for the authenticity of her own voice. I am sure *Through the Fire* will transform your life, just as it has opened up mine to greater self-acceptance, inner peace and unconditional love.

Wishing the same for each of you,

Ginger Merrill Perlman

Introduction

> "I found I could say things with color and shapes that
> I couldn't say any other way – things I had no words for."
> – *Georgia O'Keefe, Artist*

Venus of Willendorf

Over 30 thousand years ago, our earliest ancestor Cro-Magnon man (or woman) picked up a stone and began chipping away at a chunk of unformed rock. The result may have been the tiny limestone sculpture affectionately termed *Venus of Willendorf* found in a fertile valley of lower Austria and believed to be the oldest surviving piece of prehistoric art. Not surprisingly, this earliest statue dating back to approximately 24,000 BCE, depicts a woman. The sculptor was clearly paying tribute to the female's goddess-like power of reproduction as shown by her pendulous breasts, fruitful belly and swollen vulva. Before ancient humans understood the science behind the birds and the bees, a woman's ability to bring forth life was seen as magic of the highest order! Today, artists are still paying homage to the miracle of the female goddess.

From the beginning of time, art has fulfilled our human need to make sense of the mystifying world around us. It also gives us a creative outlet for expressing our deepest dreams and desires, as well as our greatest fears and failures. Creating art is a birthing of oneself – giving life to the subconscious and subjective expressions of our soul. It is enlightening to discover what this "inner" mind has to say, since the artful journey we are now on is all about enlightenment.

Working as a psychotherapist for over 30 years, I have experienced the similarities in the process of creating ceramic art and the process of personal growth. My professional career began as an art therapist, followed later by training and certification as a psychodramatist. For many years, I worked in psychiatric hospitals helping patients use both art and drama as a means of expressing their innermost thoughts and feelings. It worked. In most cases, they started seeing themselves more clearly and objectively, and began to change and to heal.

After fifteen years of teaching others personal growth and transformation through art, I entered a dark period of my own soul. I experienced a series of traumatic life changes – surviving a difficult divorce, becoming a single mom and undergoing a complete hysterectomy. Each of these challenges provided extraordinary life lessons. That is when I began working with clay and the process became my mirror, my healer.

Like our own material bodies, clay is composed of earth elements and when mixed with water, it takes on a life of its own. Much like the way we shape our own destinies, the artist shapes, forms and decorates this raw material. She then releases it into the fire where it transforms once again. The sculptor must now decide the best way to honor her work of art, just as we must learn how to honor ourselves. I use the process of creating ceramic art as a metaphor for how we interpret our changing life's experience. To simplify the process of creating ceramic art, I have separated it into five stages of transformation – Preparing, Producing, Firing, Finishing and Freeing. These stages can be likened to the five passages each woman goes through as she transforms her consciousness to the Wise Woman. In this process, she is creating her own greatest work of art – herself.

Each stage of our life, including the bumps and cracks we must endure along with the triumphs, builds the necessary foundation to get us to the next phase. The same holds true for clay making. Although some of our creations may not turn out the way we had intended, these "accidents" always prove to be valuable learning experiences. It is only through both our mistakes and our successes that we learn to make the next piece even better.

That is what this process is all about – change. Recognizing the perfect order of it all, especially if a particular piece or period in life seems quite imperfect, is one of our greatest challenges. Conscious awareness is required to accept both the pleasure and the pain we encounter along our journey and to appreciate the value of both in helping us grow.

So whether or not you have ever worked with clay, picked up a paintbrush or scribbled with a crayon, it really doesn't matter, because YOU are the art form and YOU are the artist of yourself.

The ceramic art I have created over the past 15 years is displayed on the following pages and reflects my own soul's journey towards self-expression and transformation. It is my intention that this expression will serve as a guidepost to help you gain conscious awareness of where you have been, where you are now and where you may be headed on your own journey of transformation. At times you may imagine that you are stuck at one stage along the way, but remember that you can always turn to the next page and see the possibilities that lie ahead.

To enhance your interactive experience with this book, please use the following "Five Rs:"

- Read the text.
- React to the art.
- Relate your own thoughts, feelings and memories in the self-help worksheets.
- Recognize old restrictive/dysfunctional belief systems and behaviors.
- Resolve to transform old interpretations into new positive perspectives.

If any of the photos or your answers to the questionnaires cause you to feel uneasy or resistant, please remember that feelings of resistance often herald change. So as we begin this journey together, keep in mind, it is only through our willingness to go in to the fire; to experience the discomfort of self-observation, that we alone birth our conscious choices to transform into our own magnificent works of art.

Like any art project, our lives are built upon layers, textures and colors of our unique experiences. This book too builds upon its previous chapter. No matter how many chapters we have in our life, with careful attention and commitment to each stage of personal growth, we can become that peaceful Wise Woman who lies sleeping in the raw clay of our hearts and minds.

Stage One

Maidening - *Preparing*

Chapter 1

The Age of Formation

"The emotional, sexual and psychological stereotyping of females begins when the doctor says, "It's a girl."
Shirley Chisholm, first African-American Congresswoman

We all come from Mother Earth and we all return to her. Our bodies are composed of the same earth elements as clay and when these elements are mixed with the right proportions of water, we start to take shape.

The artist starts out with a desire, a feeling, or a vision of what her piece may become. She must perceive it in the clay first and then transform this expression of her inner mind into a physical reality outside of herself.

Anyone who has ever worked with ceramics will tell you that one of the most vital steps in creating a successful work of art is the proper preparation of the clay. The clay starts out with many irregularities; it may contain air pockets, small rocks or impurities, and may be too wet or too dry. All of these inconsistencies need to be pounded, kneaded, patted, folded and smoothed out repeatedly by the artist to finally obtain the desired uniformity of the clay.

We, too, start out from a "desire" and gradually take material form, first in the womb and later in life. Each of us is molded and shaped by the people, society and environment around us until we are finally able to stand on our own. If not given the proper nurturing, nutrition and knowledge in our formative years, we may suffer the same fate as a badly formed piece of pottery – if too dry, it may crack; if too wet, it may wobble and if the air bubbles or impurities are never smoothed out, the pot may explode when placed in the fire.

How well we turn out psychologically usually depends on how well we are handled. From the start, each of us is as soft and malleable as clay. We are "kneaded" into shape by our families, teachers, religions and nationalities. It is also important to have a stable base from which to start this shaping, but sometimes because of imbalances or irregularities, the form doesn't turn out the way we intended. We need the proper space, correct tools and the gentle, but firm hands of experience to guide us into our optimal shapes.

Working with clay is one pathway to self-discovery. The artist does not experience her art as "it" is, but as "she" is. Depending upon her own personal interpretation, she feels and creates that which speaks from her heart, body and mind. Philosopher Suzanne K. Langer sums it up with, "Art is the objectification of feeling."

Maidening - Preparing

In art, as in life, what we think is often what we experience, and what an artist thinks she is creating in the moment, may speak differently to her as she grows and evolves. In our transformational growth, our life becomes our own interpretation and our own work of art.

The clay pieces that you will see throughout this book are the products of my own journey towards conscious awareness. They are my "babies" and each one is a reflection of me at a different milepost along my way. Through my art, I began the process of freeing my soul, claiming my heart and becoming one with my Higher Self. It is my hope that these clay sculptures will also serve as catalysts for your own interpretation, personal growth and self-discovery.

After years of helping others express themselves through art, I finally started using this process for myself. I signed up for a clay class - the first one I had taken in more than thirty years – which met deep in the woods of upstate New York. Our first assignment was to dig our own potting clay from the earth, then to gather rocks to build an outdoor kiln.

Our instructor asked us to create two separate pieces that were not alike, but worked together as a pair. I took the wet, smooth clay into my hands and allowed myself to be at one with it. The creations that came out of this experience are called *In the Beginning* (fig. 1 – below). As you can see, the piece on the left is shorter and has smooth circular shapes surrounding a cave-like hollow. The piece on the right is larger, more upright and has fluid wave-like forms that fit into the cave. Together the shapes flow into each other; one being inner and the other being outer.

Fig. 1 - In the Beginning

The Age of Formation

During the time that I created these sculptures, I was studying and writing about the feminine and masculine aspects found in every human. These pieces were not intended to represent man or woman, but rather the energies that are present in each individual. In much of my work I have used body parts to symbolize these aspects. Eastern philosophies have recognized these principles for thousands of years and refer to the female energy as "yin" and the male energy as "yang." In the womb before our gender has been defined, we contain both principles equally. After birth, those energies begin to distinguish themselves, yet continue to ebb and flow throughout life. As we mature, the most balanced of us learn how to successfully integrate and honor both of those parts within.

Another early sculpture, Egg Girl (fig. 2 – below), also embraces this initial phase of feminine formation. This piece reminds me of an egg and the Raku finish I chose has a crackled look resembling the shell of an egg as it crackles to let the life inside emerge. What we see first about this piece (and what we see first about each other) is the shell we all wear on the outside. Either we like it or we don't.

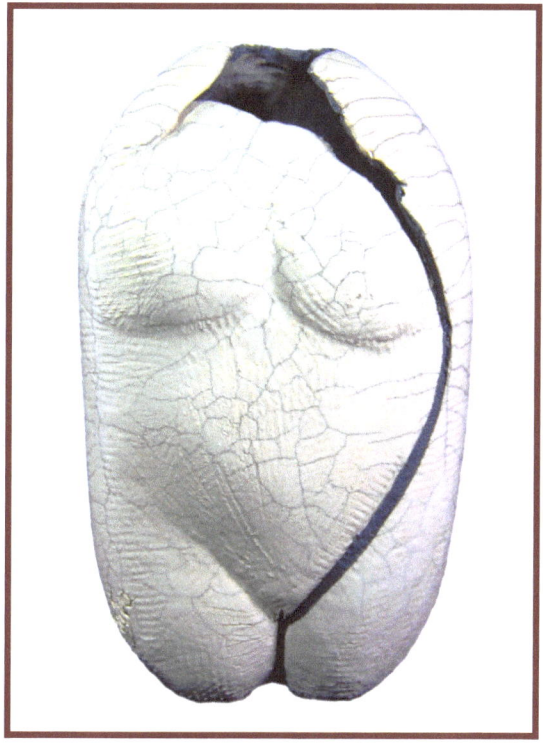

Fig. 2 - Egg Girl

The black line that winds up the side of this sculpture represents the Kundalini (life force) energy flowing through her and up into the opening at the top. Each child enters this world with her skull still soft on top, as if she were still connected to the source from which she comes. According to a school of yoga that originated in the 11th century AD, Kundalini is said to rise upward, piercing the six chakra centers until reaching the seventh chakra in the crown of the head. It is then believed to connect in a spiritual union with a Divine Energy Source.

Maidening - Preparing

Egg Girl is smooth and unformed, ready to be shaped by the world around her and, like most of my creations, is an empty vessel waiting to be filled.

In this next sculpture, *Opening* (fig. 3 – below), my intention was to capture the innocence of unfolding and looking out into the world as new. This young girl is a flower blooming and I chose to glaze her face golden to reflect her angelic qualities that are as pure and as precious as gold. There is a naiveté about her as she peers out of her vessel-like body, waiting to be filled or put to use. Her form is glazed a soft shade of green – the color of the first leaves to open in early spring. At this stage of formation, the girl is quickly blossoming into a young woman and still has the golden glow of hopeful expectancy and wonder on her upturned face.

Fig. 3 – Opening

During this earliest period of development, many of our personal belief systems are being formed. A belief system is a core set of values and rules stored in our subconscious mind through which we filter the experiences and information we gain throughout our lives. Like a computer, our subconscious sorts this "data" into files and labels each experience as good or bad, safe or dangerous, depending upon our unique circumstances. These foundational belief systems are created from birth, and many psychologists think they may start forming in *utero*.

The Age of Formation

Our subconscious mind, also like a computer, "programs" our behavior in response to these belief systems. Our beliefs form a framework that prescribes our actions, our conduct and our perspectives on life. A complex set of emotions is stored along with each of our belief systems, and since we are usually unaware of the source of these feelings or beliefs, we assume "they" are "us." It is through this subconscious programming that we learn to identify ourselves by our feelings, experiences, stories and beliefs.

For example, if a little girl has a domineering, critical or punitive parent, she may think "I can't do this myself," or "I am wrong," or "I am bad". Using our computer analogy, each belief is stored in "files" of emotions, such as fear, doubt or shame. Later in life, the girl may adapt coping behaviors based on these beliefs such as becoming a helpless victim (fear), withdrawing from interaction (doubt), or allowing others to mistreat or abuse her (shame).

From this very same programming and fear base, the young girl may have formed a coping technique of abandoning others. Instead of thinking, "I can't do this alone," she believes, "I don't need anyone's help." Instead of feeling "I am wrong," she asserts, "It's my way or the highway," and instead of internalizing, "I am bad," she stores the belief, "I can't trust anyone."

Whichever method of coping techniques we adopt, we keep our initial belief systems formed in childhood intact and go through life justifying them. Only by becoming consciously aware of our core beliefs – and the feelings and behaviors that stem from them – can we assess, accept and adjust them to transform into our true Authentic Self, and awaken our Wise Woman which is our goal.

To better understand this concept, the following chart defines both the "positive" (expanding) and "negative" (contracting) behavior characteristics of the Inner Child. Throughout this book, you will see this term referred to frequently.

THE INNER CHILD - Positive and Negative Behavior Characteristics

Positive (Authentic) – Expanding	Negative (Learned) - Contracting
Innocent	Self-doubting
Spontaneous	Inhibited
Sexually free	Sexually repressed
Expressive	Non-communicative
Playful	Withdrawn
Full of self-worth	Unworthy/shameful
Open to love	Unloved/unloving
Seeks attention	Hides
Wants to participate	Acts out
Trusting	Distrusting
Confident	Inadequate

The Inner Child is a *persona* or identity we will carry with us throughout our lifetime, no matter what chronological age we may reach. The goal is to recognize this voice and to respond to her words and requests in an increasingly disciplined and conscious way.

In Summary

The Age of Formation creates the foundation upon which the rest of our life rests. Our lifelong beliefs and attitudes are shaped during this formative time. If we were not given the love, attention or guidance we needed as we were forming, we may enter the next phase of transformation, young womanhood, lacking the inner strength to express, protect and develop our true Authentic Self. By this time, most of us have learned and integrated some negative beliefs about ourselves, which lead to the contraction of our more positive and expansive authentic Inner Child.

However, possibilities always exist for change.

If our earliest environment was solid and supportive where love and acceptance flowed easily, we have a good chance of moving into the next stage, the Age of Attraction, whole and unscarred with our authentic Inner Child relatively intact.

Chapter 2

The Age of Attraction

"The hunger for love is much more difficult to remove than the hunger for bread."
Mother Teresa, Humanitarian and recipient of The Nobel Peace Prize

As the maiden enters this phase of her journey of transformation, she is undergoing dramatic physical changes. Her body is rapidly developing into a woman, but her emotions and sense of reason lag far behind. Although the teenage girl is now all dressed up in the garb of womanhood, she still remains childlike.

During this period of discovery, our imaginations are filled with colorful dreams and far-fetched fantasies; however, we lack the experience to see the truth of our realities. We are eager to test our newly-formed wings of womanhood, but haven't yet gained the maturity to recognize how fragile they really are. The maiden is caught in an uncomfortable tug of war between her desire for independence and her need for dependency. She ventures forth with a show of bravado and unrealized confidence, only to pull back for protection when the going gets rough.

This early stage of personal transformation can be compared to a similar process in clay making. Once the clay has been properly prepared, it is ready to be molded into its intended form. When the artist has finished the shaping, she places the clay in a safe place where it is allowed to dry slowly to partial hardness. This stage is referred to as "leatherhard," because the clay has stiffened, yet retains some of its pliancy. This is an excellent time to refine the piece by carving in decorative details and adding the finishing touches that can make it attractive.

At this stage, just like the clay, a young woman's body has grown into its intended form, but her mind is still pliant enough to be further altered by the people and pressures of her surroundings. If the clay becomes too dry at this point, it can no longer be carved. If the woman has "hardened" prematurely from negative experiences, she has little flexibility to bounce back and may be permanently wounded. She then may lack the resilience she needs to move forward in a more positive direction.

One of the artist's goals in creating her art is to attract. She may wish to lure a buyer, gain recognition for her talent or draw attention to her subject matter. The same holds true for the maiden at this stage. She may flaunt her blossoming sexuality in hopes of attracting a mate or protector, or show off her talents, abilities or charms to get what she wants from her teachers, employers, family or friends.

Maidening - Preparing

This is a period of ongoing exploration, but first the young woman must separate from her parents so she may attract other connections. A new bond may take the form of a romantic connection, or it may take the shape of a cause or a cult. All of these connections are subject to rapid change, because just as a teenager frequently changes her clothing to suit her whim or the latest trend, maidens also try on different identities at this stage. A dilemma occurs when she tries to forge an independent identity while still being tied to the apron strings of dependency. As much as her cocky persona may shout independence, the seemingly self-assured maiden is still shadowed by her lurking fear of abandonment.

Fig. 4 – Pretty Butt Naive

To illustrate this ongoing struggle between naïveté and maturity in the maiden, I created *Pretty Butt Naïve* (Fig. 4 – above). In this sculpture, the female figure is all dressed up in a butterfly dress with glorious wings outstretched in back. Seen from the front, we notice her beautiful breasts, her slinky figure and her proud and haughty stance. I chose a shiny bronze Raku finish for this dress to mirror the maiden's brassy confidence and hauteur.

The Age of Attraction

However, if you turn the sculpture around you see that the butterfly's cocoon is still opening and unknown to the cheeky young woman inside, her cute little naked butt is showing! Not only does this reflect her girlish innocence, but also her vulnerable openness to both the risks and the potentials of the world around her.

Look again at the figure and you will notice that she lacks another very significant feature - a head. At this stage of her transformation, the maiden is focused on her body and its feelings, as well as what her peers have to say. She has little accuracy of vision as mindfulness has yet to develop. As she proudly marches into life with her new grown-up body, the maiden has scant knowledge of her limited awareness or how silly she may appear to others.

Interestingly enough, this age of attraction has nothing to do with chronological age. There are many women in their 50's and older who still haven't taken off their ribbons or bows, continue to talk in their little girl voices, ask to be saved, and walk around with their not-so-little butts showing!

The title of this next piece, *I Can Do It Any/way* (Fig. 5 – below), has two distinctly different interpretations. This sculpture can be used as a single candle holder when it stands on the young woman's legs or as a double candle holder when it is turned upside down onto its head. The maiden is so eager to please others and to be loved; she "can do it any way."

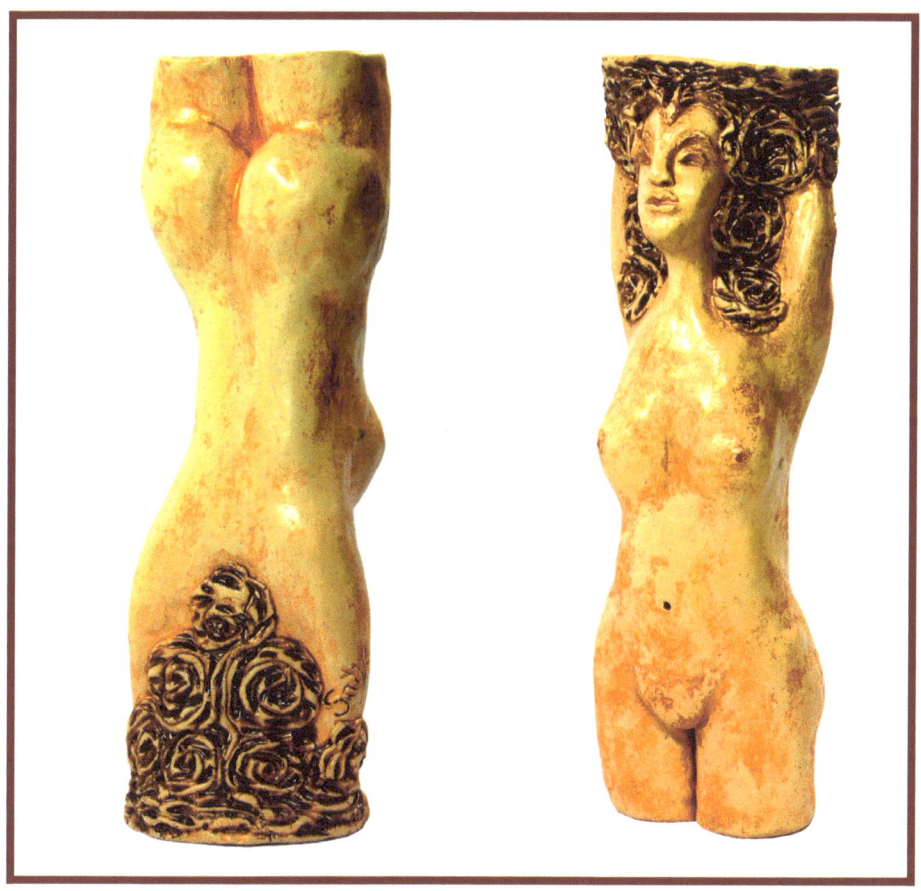

Fig. 5 – I Can Do It Any/way

This desire to be loved and wanted by others is a hallmark of this stage of transformation. The maiden measures her own self-worth by gaining others' approval, but thinks she must first prove her value to them, even if it requires that she stand on her head.

Despite the frequent neediness and acting out expressed at this stage, there is also a great deal of growing independence, which is how I arrived at the second meaning of the title, *I Can Do It Any/way*. In this version, it is as if the hardening young woman is saying, "I don't need your permission, thank you very much, because I am in charge here. Just look at how talented, unique and capable I am." By this point, the young woman is starting to feel the power of her own attractiveness or individuality and attempts to manipulate it to her full advantage.

Driven by her contradictions at this stage, it is as if the maiden is pleading "Need me, love me, want me," on one hand, while screaming "Screw you, leave me alone" on the other. She hasn't yet learned to balance these two conflicting aspects of her being, as balance is a part of wisdom still far beyond her grasp. Instead, the maiden will flip back and forth, sending out mixed messages in the process, as she tries to burn her candle at both ends.

During this period of transformation, the Inner Child discussed in Chapter 1 is joined by another lifelong persona, which I call the "Inner Teen." This rebellious and adventuresome new identity emerges to protect the powerless Inner Child and their codependent relationship continues throughout life. The contracted Inner Teen is always trying to prove something and frequently finds fault, blames others, and uses defensiveness as a shield to protect her vulnerability. The following chart will help to clarify the differences between the positive and negative behavior characteristics of this reactive Inner Teen.

THE INNER TEEN - Positive and Negative Behavior Characteristics

Positive (Authentic) – Expanding	**Negative (Learned) - Contracting**
Adventuresome	Fearful
Independent	Conformist
Creative	Shut-down
Sexually curious/explorative	Sexually inhibited/promiscuous
Self-confident	Self-doubting/loathing
Motivated to succeed	Avoids/denies
Sets healthy limits	Lacks healthy boundaries
Socially cooperative	Uncooperative /blaming
Strives for connection	Separates

The Age of Attraction

Despite the turmoil of both the Inner Child and Inner Teen within her, the maiden continues to grow into the strength of her feminine energy/ attractiveness. She is becoming empowered by her successes at either attracting a lover, finding a rescuer, impressing a boss or getting accepted into college. Her beauty, talents or abilities have started to reap their desired rewards and with this awareness comes power.

Typically, power is associated with the male energy "yang" in Eastern philosophy, as opposed to its yielding female counterpart, "yin." At this level of transformation, we are starting to recognize the male energy in ourselves. However, we are still more interested in *attracting* that power to us, rather than *developing* it from within.

A power play between these two energies can be seen in the following piece, *Cocksure* (fig. 6 – below). Here we see the maiden sitting confidently upon a pedestal, one foot planted on top of the world, her elbow resting nonchalantly on the huge book of man's history. We can see by her rather masculine posture that she has nothing to hide – she is proud, self-assured and feels empowered by her "yin" energy.

Fig.6 – Cocksure

Maidening - Preparing

Upon closer observation, you will notice that several erect penises support the pedestal upon which she sits. This cocksure young woman feels superior to and in control of the male energy beneath her. She is unaware that she gained her dominant attitude through feminine manipulation, since she lacks the physical strength to gain it otherwise. Whether this female persuasion took the shape of sexual favors, servitude, charm, hard work or mental acuity – it really doesn't matter. She believes the balance of power has shifted her way and the maiden may now reap the rewards she desires.

Emboldened by her newly found strengths, this cocky young woman feels on top of the world. The earth is there for her taking as it spins beneath her feet. At this stage of her journey, the maiden fantasizes that she can do it all, get it all, and give to all. She has embraced the power of her "yin" energy and has begun to use the "yang" within herself as well.

Despite all her bravado, the maiden leans for support upon the book of "history" which provides her foundation. How the maiden defines herself today is based upon these predominantly male writings – "his" story, not hers – that have shaped human civilization for the past 4,000 years. Prior to that, there had been a Goddess culture that revered the power of the feminine in all aspects of life, but male-dominated religions put an end to it. For the past several thousand years, women have been subjugated to male energy and "his" stories have been handed down for generations to our maiden.

Although the young woman in this sculpture seems cocksure of herself, hers is a false and fleeting bravado. The glass ceiling for females still exists in the 21st century, but this grandiose maiden is still too naïve to understand her culturally-imposed gender challenges.

In the next sculpture from the Age of Attraction, we now see the maiden *Waiting for the Groom* (fig. 7 – following page). This sweet young woman is patiently waiting for the perfect partner - be it a man or a woman, the perfect career, or a two-story house in the suburbs. It matters little what form this connection takes. What does matter is the maiden's inability to realize that perfection will never come. Perfection exists only in the dictionary, so seeking it will only lead to disillusionment and disappointment.

Looking at this sculpture, you will see that the maiden is holding a bouquet in her arms. Upon closer inspection, you will observe that the flower is a "perfect" penis, symbolizing the perfection for which she strives. This phallic flower also suggests that the young woman still believes that she draws her yang energy from without, instead of developing it from within.

Turning again to the sculpture, you will see a frilled opening on the woman's right side. This empty space (in actuality, a candle holder) is where her perfect groom – fantasy or dream – is supposed to go. She waits to have this hollow filled with her expectations of who (or what) she thinks she needs, wants and deserves at this stage of her journey. All of these "supposed to be's" spring from her ever-evolving sense of self. Still too naïve to doubt that all of her wishes will come true, this bride will continue to wait in vain, expectantly scanning the future for her perfect life.

The Age of Attraction

Fig. 7 – Waiting for the Groom

In Summary

The Age of Attraction is a time of transition from the innocence of girlhood to the experiences of womanhood. The maiden dons the body of a woman, but remains childlike in many ways. This is a period of discovery, dreams and fantasies blended with a growing awareness of the realities of the world. The young woman puts on a show of dramatic confidence in her quest for independence, which dimly masks her underlying need for dependency.

Despite her persona of cocky self-assurance, the maiden is often plagued by self-consciousness and neediness at this stage. These feelings are acted out through mixed messages, blame and victimization. Her quest to be loved and needed can also lead her to inappropriate choices. If unable to attract the attention, affection and protection she wants, the maiden's fear of abandonment can lead to depression, substance abuse, or sexual promiscuity.

However, possibilities always exist for change.

If the young woman channels her energy and growing self-confidence into positive ways, she can blossom into an independent, accomplished individual. At this stage of her journey, the maiden is adventuresome, enthusiastic, creative and playful – all valuable qualities to carry into her adult life. She has embraced the power of her femininity, whether she consciously knows this or not, and is becoming aware of the strength of the male energy within herself, as well. As the maiden approaches her next stage of transformation, Mothering, she will decorate herself with all of the beliefs, skills and experiences she has learned so far.

Self-Help Worksheet
Stage One: Maidening - *Preparing*

Now that you have completed reading Stage One, it is *your* turn to respond to the artwork. Take time to meditate on each photograph and think about how the pieces speak to you. Your written expression of how you relate to them is extremely important. You will gain more self-awareness by doing so and become more conscious of where you are in your own journey of transformation. Spend 30 seconds or so reacting to the art before answering the following questions. Use a separate sheet of paper for each photograph, if needed.

Remember, your first impressions are often the most important ones and there are no right answers!

SELF-HELP EXERCISE:

What would you name this piece if you were the sculptor?

_____
_____
_____
_____
_____
_____

What feelings, sensations or emotions does this piece evoke in you?

_____
_____
_____
_____
_____
_____

Maidening - Preparing

What scenes or memories from your life does this piece help you recall?

_____
_____
_____
_____
_____
_____

What thoughts or beliefs about your life come to mind while looking at this piece?

_____
_____
_____
_____
_____

If you don't like it, why not?

_____
_____
_____
_____

If you do like it, why?

_____
_____
_____
_____

Four A's
Self-Help Worksheet
Stage One: Maidening - *Preparing*

After completing the SELF-HELP WORKSHEET, please reflect upon what you may have learned about yourself from these exercises. It is now your opportunity to put this awareness into action. Take all the time you need to answer the following questions thoughtfully and *honestly*. Use separate sheets of paper, if necessary:

1. AWARENESS

What negative beliefs about yourself have you held onto from this "Preparing" stage of your life? (Example: *"I am not worthy of love."*)

_____
_____
_____
_____
_____
_____

What positive beliefs about yourself do you have from this "Preparing" stage? (Example: *"I am adventuresome."*)

_____
_____
_____
_____
_____
_____

2. ACCEPTANCE

What are you willing to accept as "authentic" beliefs about yourself from this stage?

_____
_____
_____
_____
_____
_____
_____

3. ACTION

What old or dysfunctional beliefs and feelings about yourself are you willing to release?

_____
_____
_____
_____
_____

What negative behaviors and habits are you willing to let go of?

_____
_____
_____
_____
_____
_____

4. APPRECIATION

Make a Gratitude List of the things you appreciate about yourself from this stage.

_____
_____
_____
_____
_____
_____
_____

What new beliefs will you mold for yourself from this gratitude list?

_____
_____
_____
_____
_____
_____
_____
_____

What new behaviors will you decorate yourself with and embrace?

_____
_____
_____
_____
_____
_____
_____
_____

Stage Two

Mothering - *Producing*

Chapter 3

The Age of Attachment

"Who so loves, believes the impossible."
Elizabeth Barrett Browning, Poet of the Victorian Era

Once the maiden connects with her lover, her career or her cause, the stage of mothering begins. Mothering is a time of establishing emotional bonds and connections and nurturing the support and sustenance gained through them. This is a period when a woman desires being needed. She wants to give to others and often defines her self-worth by how much she can please, fix or help them. She accepts this as her duty and responsibility and devotes most of her energy to caring for the needs and demands of her "other," be it a mate, a boss, an organization, or an issue.

The young woman is very much like the clay at this stage of transformation. The decorative touches have been added to the piece and it has not entirely hardened. The pottery is now referred to as greenware, because although it has taken on its intended form, it can still be broken, softened with water and kneaded back into a malleable lump of clay. At this point, the clay is in a passive state awaiting its first firing, but there has been no permanent transformation in its chemical composition.

Women, like the clay, are partially hardened at this point. We have formulated belief systems and coping techniques about who we are and what works for us, and have become "brittle" attached to these identities. However, many of us have experienced being "broken" and reformed during this secondary stage of development. In our need for validation, some of us have gone so far as to deny our own Authentic Self to assume the shape that suits someone else.

This willful self-sacrifice can be seen in the following sculpture, *Anything to Please* (fig.8 – following page). Despite her bending-over-backwards pose, the woman in this piece has a smile of serene contentment on her face. Her dress of changing colors has a scaly, snake-like quality and she can shed her own skin and twist into the new shapes others may ask of her. Also like a snake, this female lacks arms and is unable to reach for her own needs or legs to take her where she independently wants to go. Instead, the lovely lady stays grounded on her gilded pedestal, waiting for others to bend her at will.

Why, then, is she smiling? At this stage of personal growth, a woman is focused outward and derives a great deal of gratification from serving the real or perceived needs of others. In return for her efforts, she may gain the love and support of a mate, the financial reward of an employer, or the trust of a friend. A symbiosis is formed from these attachments that allow women to create families, build productive careers, or establish empathetic bonds of friendship.

Fig. 8 – Anything to Please

From early childhood on, our culture conditions girls to believe that there are big rewards for those who are pleasing in appearance or action, and preferably, in both. The traditional roles of daughter, mate and mother are defined by our patriarchal society and fed by the fantasy that it is selfish to say no. A woman who takes care of her needs first is perceived as being self-centered, while a man who does the same, is viewed as self-sufficient. Many girls are taught to be obedient, cute and helpful, while little boys are usually praised for their intelligence, bravery and competitive spirit. Is it any wonder that we grow up viewing our own self-worth upside-down through the eyes of others?

The Age of Attachment

Although much of this care-taking belief system grows from our cultural roots, there is also a biological component to the female's desire to give. Women are nurturers by nature, so it is instinctive for us to focus our energies on the needs of others. In the next sculpture, *Holding Time*, we see a woman "pregnant" with all of the attachments that she wants to hold and to grow in the hollow of her waiting open arms. Her sweet face smiles out from the deep recesses of her hood - her identity nearly hidden in deference to the open "nest" below. Her loving embrace gently cradles all that she has worked so hard to nurture, be it a life partner, a child, her profession or a cause. Her own individuality is camouflaged here, as suggested by the plain white robe that nearly hides her face in the background.

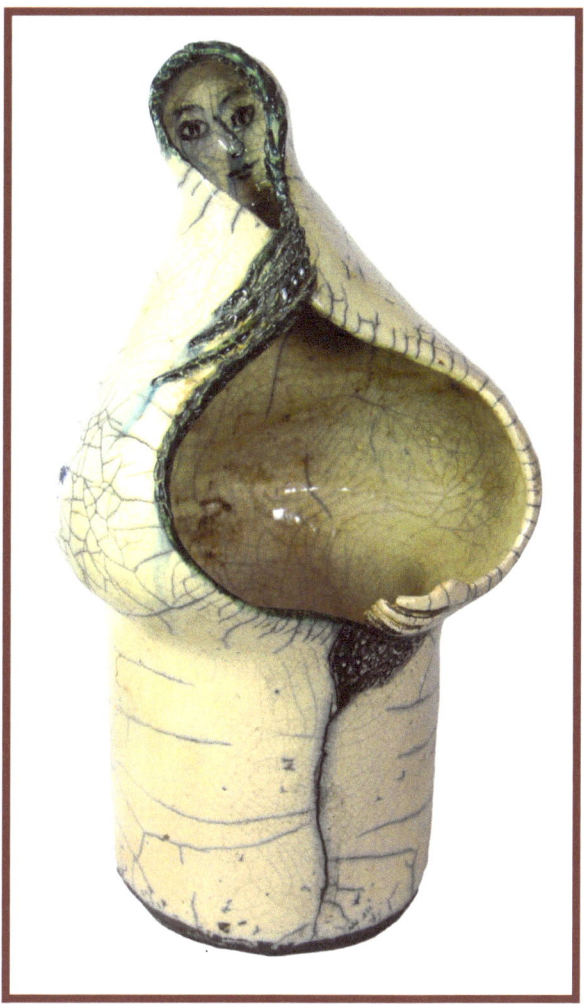

Fig. 9 - Holding Time

There may be a great deal of subservience seen in this piece, yet also something quite noble. Humility is a necessary part of finding balance in selfhood. There is a deep satisfaction to be gained from serving others and belonging to someone or something outside of ourselves that we can call our own.

Although there is a definite value to acts of giving, the individual must carefully control her selflessness by establishing healthy boundaries for herself. For many women, however, this delicate balancing act often tips in favor of the "other." She may neglect her own physical, spiritual or emotional well-being in the process, creating a vicious cycle of fatigue, irritability and depression. The more she grows to love and identify with her attachments, the more she may ignore her own needs, dreams and truths.

In Summary

The Age of Attachment is a time of forming significant interpersonal bonds with a mate, child, boss or cause. The focus of these relationships is outward for most women, placing the needs of the other over the needs of self. Many of us were taught that it is selfish to focus attention on ourselves, so regardless of the sacrifices required of us, we tend to make the expectations of others our priorities.

For most women, this need to nurture takes the form of the maternal instinct and finds fulfillment in motherhood. Equally as strong in others, this drive finds expression in "nurturing" a partner, an employer, pets, friends, extended family members or volunteer causes. The ability for a "mother" to care for the life she creates is both a model for most human relationships, as well as the foundation for all human society.

With this gift of selfless giving, however, comes the potential for giving ourselves away in the process. For many women, their attachments gain such importance they no longer realize where their own boundaries end and the "others" begin. Without a healthy balance between her inner and outer worlds, the young woman may enter the next phase, the Age of Selflessness, with very little self-esteem or authenticity left intact.

However, possibilities always exist for change.

If at this point in her transformation, the woman has developed a positive self-image along with the ability to know her boundaries and to speak her truth, her desire to serve will continue to foster personal growth. Her willingness to nurture will help her put down roots, build a stable family unit, and help all the people and projects she cares about without diminishing her own sense of Self.

Chapter 4

The Age of Selflessness

"The woman is uniformly sacrificed to the wife and mother."
Elizabeth Cady Stanton, Women's Rights Activist (1815-1902)

=

At this stage of transformation, the "mother" has become so closely bonded to her mate or partner, her growing family, a cause or career, she may lose sight of her own personal needs and wants. Although she draws satisfaction and sustenance from these attachments, she may forsake her own sense of Self in her efforts to help, fix, nurture, teach and grow the "others." Her life revolves around those on the outside and she may find herself identifying with or "becoming" them.

This pattern of bonded attachment is typical for most women. However, others follow a different path of "mothering." These individuals did not receive the essential nurturing they needed during their Age of Formation years. This emotional absence or neglect at such an early stage of development may have led to deep scars of rejection that bar these women from the "holding" phase of traditional motherhood.

Instead of wanting to nurture and serve others, these women recoil from selfless giving and focus on protecting themselves. Instead of asking, "What can I do for you?" they wonder, "What can I get from you?" as they continue their subconscious search for a mother figure. Instead of wishing to hold others close, these women keep them at arm's length. This distancing technique of "Notice me, but stay away," allows them to believe subconsciously that by thwarting intimacy they will be shielded from rejection. Ironically, the "abandoned" have now become the "abandoners."

At this time of scant self-awareness, the givers and the takers seem to be quite different from each other; however, both types are moving in opposite directions away from their true Authentic Selves. Paradoxically, the same life events can lead different women to follow either one of these divergent paths. Our belief systems are affected not only by the age at which these life events occur, but also by our birth order in the family.

For example, a younger victim of emotional neglect may believe, "Nobody is paying attention to me, so I'll do whatever I want," while her older sibling may think, "Nobody seems to be watching out for us, so I have to take care of the others." While the younger child may never develop the desire to nurture or trust others, her sister may be unable to stop giving or to accept others' love. These two examples may seem extreme to most of us, since the majority of women fall somewhere between the givers and the takers.

Mothering - Producing

In the following sculpture which is my favorite piece, *Our Lady of Perpetual Giving* (fig. 10 – below), I tried to capture the inner savior that many women feel at this chapter in their lives. Notice that her face wears a serene expression of resignation and acceptance with her role in life. Her head is bowed in a gesture of surrender and she is at peace.

Fig. 10 – Our Lady of Perpetual Giving

The Age of Selflessness

Our lady's skin is smoked to resemble the dark and light hide of a Guernsey cow – and also like this gentle animal – her body is covered with many milk-giving teats or breasts. Her posture is one of ultimate self-sacrifice being nailed to her red (savior) cross of martyrdom. She lives only to serve and invites all those that wish, to come suckle from her.

In addition to being immobilized by her cross of attachments, this mother also lacks arms to satisfy her own needs. At this stage of development for most women, we are still in the early years of our careers, marriages or family building, so we seem willing to accept very little in return for the privilege of holding onto our attachments.

At some point in time, this total commitment to doing for others takes its toll. In the next sculpture *Hanging On* (fig. 11 – below), the figure is clinging onto the world she has created for herself. Like a fallen angel, her wings have collapsed and she is lying there exhausted and spent. Her limp posture reflects an "I've had it and can't keep it up anymore" sort of attitude.

Fig. 11 – Hanging On

Mothering - Producing

Perhaps she hates her dead-end job, but still can't leave it; perhaps her kids are growing up, but she refuses to let them go, or maybe the love has gone out of her marriage, yet she still hangs on to it.

Despite our exhaustion at this phase of our transformation, many of us still cling to the old belief that we can and are supposed to fix it all and make it right, be it personal, professional or even societal. Whether this need to fix things comes from a place of true compassion and selflessness, or is motivated by a desire for personal attention and recognition really doesn't matter. The energy expended and the exhaustion that follows is the same, regardless of the motivation.

Returning to the sculpture, we can think of this figure as the Super Woman of today who manages to juggle it all – family, work and volunteer organizations – until one day she must simply drop the ball. Her face rests in the mud of Mother Earth and unbeknown to her, she is being filled up and re-nourished by its healing female yin energy. Just as seeds must be planted in the earth to gestate, so must we return to the Mother within us to nurture ourselves and to grow.

The angel's collapse was inevitable, and it was only a matter of time before she would slip from her self-imposed pedestal of perfection. Her journey has finally arrived at a place of stasis and now she must turn inward for answers, instead of without. Despite her inertia, we see that the figure's long hair is blowing in the wind as the world continues to turn without her help. She has entered a period of deep self-reflection and healing, paving the way for the endless possibilities that lie ahead.

In Summary

The Age of Selflessness is a phase when many women possess little of their own Authentic Selves while providing for the perceived wishes, needs or demands of others. Their hope is that through their own self-sacrifice, they will be able to create the ideal conditions for mutual love to thrive, understanding to flourish, and security to grow. In their desire and expectation to love and to be loved unconditionally, to understand and to be understood intuitively, to provide and to be provided for with support and protection, women often find themselves unbalanced on the side of giving, with little getting back in return.

During this period, women frequently bounce back and forth between feeling in control and feeling helpless. We push ourselves to our limits both physically and emotionally to take care of our attachments – be it a partner, child or career – rarely realizing the toll it is taking on us. If our "Mothering" experience does not live up to our expectations, disappointment can overwhelm us leaving us feeling anxious, resentful, depressed, and confused.

However, possibilities always exist for change.

If the woman has been able to strike a healthful balance between her female yin energy (nurturing) and her male yang energy (asserting), and has created clear boundaries she will enter the next phase of transformation, Morphing, well prepared for the challenges that lie ahead. Her efforts at creating and nurturing a family, whether at home or at work, will provide a foundation of security, a feeling of belonging, and a clear sense of personal identity and purpose as she explores the endless possibilities for personal growth yet to come.

Self-Help Worksheet
Stage Two: Mothering - *Producing*

Now that you have completed reading Stage Two, it is *your* turn to respond to the artwork. Return to each photograph in this section and think about how each piece resonates with you. Spend 30 seconds or so reacting to the art before answering the following questions. Use a separate sheet of paper for each photograph, if needed.

Remember, your first impressions are often the most important ones and there are no right answers!

SELF-HELP EXERCISE:

What would you name this piece if you were the sculptor?

_____
_____
_____
_____
_____
_____
_____

What feelings, sensations or emotions does this piece evoke in you?

_____
_____
_____
_____
_____
_____

The Age of Selflessness

What scenes or memories from your life does this piece help you recall?

___

What thoughts or beliefs about your life come to mind while looking at this piece?

___

If you don't like it, why not?

___

If you do like it, why?

___

Four A's
Self-Help Worksheet
Stage Two: Mothering - *Producing*

After completing the SELF-HELP WORKSHEET, please reflect upon what you may have learned about yourself from these exercises. It is now your opportunity to put this awareness into action. Take all the time you need to answer the following questions thoughtfully and *honestly*. Use separate sheets of paper, if necessary:

1. AWARENESS

What negative beliefs about yourself have you held onto from this Mothering stage of your life? (Example: *"My needs don't matter compared to the needs of others."*)

_____
_____
_____
_____
_____
_____

What positive beliefs about yourself do you have from this Producing stage?

(Example: *"I am loving and yet set clear boundaries."*)

_____
_____
_____
_____
_____
_____

2. ACCEPTANCE

What are you willing to accept as authentic beliefs about yourself after gaining awareness from this stage of Mothering?

_____
_____
_____
_____
_____
_____

3. ACTION

What old or dysfunctional beliefs and feelings are you willing to release about yourself?

_____
_____
_____
_____
_____
_____

What negative behaviors and habits are you willing to let go of?

_____
_____
_____
_____
_____
_____

4. APPRECIATION

Make a Gratitude List of the things you appreciate about yourself from this stage.

_____
_____
_____
_____
_____
_____

What new beliefs will you mold for yourself from this list?

_____
_____
_____
_____
_____
_____

What new behaviors will you attach to yourself and embrace?

_____
_____
_____
_____
_____
_____

Stage Three

Morphing - *Firing*

Chapter 5

The Age of Discontent

"A woman's discontent increases in exact proportion to her development."

Elizabeth Cady Stanton, Women's Rights Activist (1815-1902)

Morphing, which means to change shape or form, derives from the word metamorphosis, a biological term used to describe phases in the growth of organisms. More recently, morphing has become a word associated with computer technology and refers to the process of graphically transforming one image into another. Either meaning is appropriate here, as I am using this term to describe the psychological changes a woman undergoes as she transforms her own image of herself on her path to higher consciousness.

The first phase of Morphing is a time of intense discontent when confusion, dissatisfaction, anger and anxiety replace our previous feelings of belonging and contentment. Although painful, this is a necessary period of transition when a woman must challenge many of her old belief systems and behaviors in order to transform into a truer version of her Authentic Self.

For many of us, this Age of Discontent begins when we realize that we have given ourselves away for so long, that we have become empty vessels in the process. Like most of my ceramic pieces, these vessels are intended to be emptied and filled. Women at this stage of transformation have poured themselves into their families, careers or partners with little space open for being refilled. They have become aware that many of their own personal dreams and ambitions have slowly drained away while they have been busy serving the needs or demands of others.

As our self-awareness grows, a disconnect widens between our emerging feelings and our old, familiar ways. What once brought us comfort now brings us confusion. Not only have we lost a vital connection to ourselves, but we also seem to be losing the strong connection to the people and things we love. Our children are growing up and no longer need us in the same ways; we may have hit the glass ceiling at our jobs and now we are watching younger women accept our rightful promotions, or our partners might prefer spending afternoons on the golf course rather than sharing afternoon delights with us.

For other women, the Age of Discontent arises not from giving too *much* of themselves, but from giving too *little*. After years of being directed by their aggressive yang energy, these achievement-driven women may look around their surroundings to see an abundance of material things.

However, there is a paucity of close human attachments. In their focused determination to protect and prove themselves, they may have denied their deep need for a lasting love and true human intimacy. Like their yin counterparts, they are also out of balance.

Fig. 12 – Bewilderment

Despite the way each woman arrives at this place of emptiness, we share many of the same frustrations once we get there. In the sculpture, *Bewilderment* (fig. 12 – above), we see a lovely lady all dressed up with makeup and jewelry, but nowhere to go. Her oversized feet are too heavy and cumbersome for movement, and although she has wings, they are only for decoration and will never allow flight. Many conflicting ideas and emotions are sprouting like tendrils from under her hat, as if her mind is sending out distress signals from within.

The Age of Discontent

For those of us stuck in this age of discontent, the confusion comes from the static inside our minds. Our contradictory thoughts about who we have been, who we are now, and who we hope to become are spiraling out in so many directions, it is difficult to move forward. We are giving off and getting back such mixed messages through our twisted antennae, we are incapable of taking action. Although we think we are supposed to go somewhere, we just can't figure out where that is. We are lost in a familiar world without a map.

During this frustrating time of inaction, we are rooted in the heaviness of our past and present, yet are distracted by flights of fantasy luring us towards future change. Our life is experienced through these distortions and our relationships may mirror our ambivalence, indifference, or resentment. Our inner child stubbornly clings to her fears filling our minds with thoughts like, "If I really tell them how I feel, I will hurt them, or worse yet, they won't like me and will leave!" So we rationalize away our reasons for staying stuck, living under a mask of pretense or avoidance, all the while disgusted with ourselves for our dilemma and with others for their lack of understanding.

Although it is unknown to us, something powerful and positive is happening. For perhaps the first time, we are no longer sending all of our energy outward for validation or approval. Instead, we are turning inward for answers and questioning many of our old belief systems. It is often a crisis that initiates this period of intense self-reflection, be it a serious illness, a divorce, the loss of a job or the death of a friend or family member. But no matter what ignites the spark, the woman is now preparing to jump into the fire of transformation.

In the next sculpture, *Turning Away* (fig. 13 – following page), the figure's head is looking over her shoulder, while her body stays firmly planted straight ahead. She continues to go through the daily motions of her present life, yet her mind is focused elsewhere on her imagined future.

The awkward twisting of the woman's mind and body reflects the uncomfortable separation she is experiencing between her present phony-feeling old identity and her blossoming new Authentic Self. This sensation of being "two-faced" is expressed by the statue's own visage being split down the middle – black on one side (in the dark); white on the other (seeing the light.) This seemingly irresolvable black and white thinking stirs up feelings of guilt, shame, fear, or confusion and the destructive behaviors that often ensue, such as overeating, overworking or over-pleasing.

If you look closely at the sculpture, you will notice that she has no eyes. Her mind can only fantasize about the future she longs for, and since it doesn't exist yet, there is no reality she can actually see. Not only is this woman unable to see the days ahead, she is also unable to look at the truth of her todays. By facing in another direction, she is attempting to avoid or deny the pain of her present predicament.

You also may have noticed in this sculpture, the woman's "butt" is sticking out for all to see. That is because "buts" are controlling her life at this stage. "I am here, *but* not present," "I need you, *but* want you to leave," "I love you, *but* hate you, too" are just a few of the mixed messages she sends out each day.

Morphing - Firing

All of these conflicting thoughts can lead to equally confusing behavior patterns. Despite her growing anger, good girls have been taught that this emotion is inappropriate to feel, much less, to express. So instead of letting this anger out, many of us subvert it into passive-aggressive behavior, or subtle forms of manipulation. While a fed-up wife may want to let her demanding husband know how she really feels, a good-girl wife might serve him leftovers and feign a headache as her excuse.

Fig. 13 - Turning Away

For most women trapped in this limbo-land, the more we turn towards our future, the more intolerable our present becomes. Our minds race with thoughts of escape, but there seems to be no easy exit route in sight. We feel we are caught in an endless cycle of frustration – fearing change, but unable to grow without it. Writer Marilyn Ferguson captured this dilemma in the following words:

The Age of Discontent

"It's not so much we're afraid of change, or so in love with the old ways, but it's that place in between that we fear…It's like being between trapezes. It's Linus when his blanket is in the dryer. There's nothing to hold onto."

Once the discontent has taken hold, there is no turning back the emotions. In the next sculpture, *More Than Annoyed* (fig. 14 – below), we see the head of a woman about to explode. There is a seething quality about her, as if all of the pent-up emotions, expectations and frustrations she has stifled for so long are about to come spewing out in volcanic eruption.

Fig. 14 – More Than Annoyed

Her face is a dark shade of blue reflecting the deep sadness she feels. Disappointed in herself and in others, this woman fears that most of her dreams have faded. Hurt and feeling alone, she stares straight ahead – eyes wide open – facing the harsh realities of her present life. Slowly her sadness hardens to anger as she faces all of her perceived losses … in love, family, work, health, self-esteem or power. She blames herself, as well as others, for her predicament, and with this realization comes mounting anxiety.

Morphing - Firing

The female in this sculpture is blue not only from her sadness, but also from the oppressive suffocation she feels. She has allowed the grip of expectations to choke off the vitality she needs to thrive. Unwittingly, she has played a starring role in her own tragedy and much of her pain has been self-induced.

During this uncomfortable phase of transition, another persona emerges in response to the cries of our fearful Inner Child and our rebellious Inner Teen. It is the authoritative parental voice of our harsh Inner Critic. Although she can be a powerful motivator, this invasive mind talk will drag down our self-esteem with her long list of "shoulds" and "ought tos." She speaks in directives learned from her authority figures and her warnings may include: "You should never express what you really think and feel because it will only get you into trouble," "You ought to have known better," or "You should have done it perfectly."

The ridiculing judgments of the harsh Inner Critic paralyze our true intentions and silence our authentic voices. Our attempt to ignore or disagree with her only drains our energy, for she is in control. The Inner Critic seems most anxious to get our attention when we are starting to realize and express our innermost truths. For this reason, it is crucial to accept this dictatorial part of ourselves, thank her for sharing, and then take over her driver's seat. The Wise Woman is learning to distinguish between the dictates of her relentless Inner Critic and the awakening awareness of her Authentic Self.

As the pressure builds from this ongoing struggle, an unfamiliar emotion – rage – emerges and must find its release. Bubbling up from within, the anger bursts forth from her mind in snake-like coils of molten red (passion), metallic blue (sadness/loneliness) and glowing green (jealousy/envy). This Medusa-like woman is no longer interested in just being pretty, pleasant or pleasing as her masculine energy comes spiraling out.

Overwhelmed and distressed by these powerful new feelings, the woman cannot yet understand the positive significance of her present pain. Like the snake that must first shed its skin before starting anew, we must also shed our old belief systems to reveal our true authentic nature. We feel stripped naked, vulnerable and raw before our new skin has formed, yet the power in anger is a necessary catalyst in this crucial transformation.

This pivotal about-face is fueled by an energy that comes from within instead of from without, unlike the stages that came before. At this point in our journey, we are beginning to focus on our own needs – our own goals, our own desires and our own boundaries. Although we had choices before, until we awaken our sleeping consciousness, we cannot become fully aware of our power to say yes or no for our authentic truths.

In the next sculpture, Stop! (fig. 15 – following page), we see a world composed entirely of breasts. Unlike the milk-giving glands offered up so unconditionally in Our Lady of Perpetual Giving (page 52), these breasts are protected behind a grid of golden barbed wire. Instead of implying "Come and Get It," this sculpture signals "Keep Out."

The Age of Discontent

Upon closer inspection, you will notice that the barbs of the wire are turned inward as frequently as they are turned out. Women at this phase of transformation realize that their habitual need to give to others is as powerful and potentially destructive as the habit of others to take. In order to stop this imbalance, the woman must fence in her customary behavior as much as she needs to keep others' out.

For many of us, at this crucial stage of transition, we haven't mothered ourselves enough. Most of our life-giving sustenance has gone to feeding others, while we have slowly shriveled from our own "Self" starvation.

The time has finally come to get our attachments off the teat, and redirect that fortifying energy into nurturing ourselves.

Fig. 15 – Stop!

In Summary

During the Age of Discontent, our woman finally begins to find her true authentic voice – and the sound of that voice is angry. This anger may erupt from the realization that she has given herself away to her family, a boss or an organization for so long, that they have been trained to expect it. Her anger may also be directed at our society in general that tends to objectify women. Wherever it is directed, this newly expressed anger is usually frightening and unfamiliar to her and to others.

In this first phase of Morphing, the woman's latent yang energy starts rearing its powerful head from within. In the past, her masculine energy had found expression in achieving things – being the most successful salesperson or the best hockey mom on the block. The woman obtained her power from outside herself in the form of pats on the back and other's approval. At this stage of transition, however, her energy is welling up from inside herself seeking acknowledgement and personal expression.

The danger at this point lies in becoming stuck in the endless loop of fear, denial, blame, hurt, and resentment. Some women stay frozen in this state, fantasizing that their fairy godmothers will swoop down and wave their magic wands changing everything and everyone into the way it "should" be. If a woman can't access and proclaim her anger and frustration, work through it and shed her old skin in order to start anew, she could stay trapped in this cycle of discontent forever.

However, possibilities always exist for change.

If we can move through these seemingly negative or difficult emotions during this Morphing stage, we will come to realize that they were a necessary component for our positive growth and transformation. Few understand that this uncomfortable period is a new birthing of ourselves. It is a time of differentiating; of becoming aware that we are separate from the people and things we need and love.

If we accept these painful emotions, not fight or run away from them, they will help move us from hurt to healing. Just like trying to create a new art form, we are now learning to distinguish between the judgments of our harsh Inner Critic and our inner truth. By listening to our Authentic Self, we will be better prepared to make the dark journey within that awaits us in the next Age of Cocooning.

Chapter 6

The Age of Cocooning

"With each passage of human growth, we must shed a protective structure
like a hardy crustacean. We are left exposed and vulnerable – but also
yeasty and embryonic again, capable of stretching in ways we hadn't known before."
- *Gail Sheehy, American Author and Lcturer*

Cocooning is a term I use to refer to the psychological process of social and emotional isolation that we must endure to bring about major transformations in our personal growth. This psychic withdrawal may be conscious or subconscious, but in either case, the individual must delve within herself for guidance about what will come next.

In nature, this period of significant change in both appearance and character is referred to as metamorphosis. The lowly larva morphs into a beautiful butterfly; the tadpole transforms into a frog as if by magic. This physical alteration may seem quite sudden, but it actually represents thousands of years of complex evolutionary adaptation. This magical change taking place within us can transpire in a few months for some, or it may take several years for others.

Just as the caterpillar must spin a chrysalis around itself in order to transform, each woman must also enter her own internal cocoon to evoke change. She must go within the darkness of her own psyche to begin this process of personal renewal. The wooly worm is probably unaware of the instincts prompting its self-encasement, just as we are often oblivious to the reasons behind our need to withdraw from the enmeshment with people and things we care for.

During this critical phase of transition, there is a growing awareness that big changes are coming from within us, yet they are beyond our control. This realization can fill us with confusion, sadness, anger or fear as we now step into the cramped uncertainty of the unknown.

A similar period of uncertainty and doubt also occurs during the firing stage of ceramics. The clay has air-dried completely and now is ready for the first of its two firings, known as the bisque firing. The sculpture is loaded into the kiln where temperatures will gradually reach 2,400 degrees centigrade. This causes the water content within the clay to boil and evaporate which permanently transforms the molecules in the clay.

When the sculptor locks the lid on the kiln, she has no guarantee that her beloved creation will survive the intense pressures within. If it can take the heat, her sculpture will emerge permanently transformed. If the temperature rises too quickly, however, her work could explode. Despite the risks involved, the sculptor realizes her piece would be incomplete without them. There would be no glaze finish without the fire, and the glaze is what gives the sculpture its impermeable character and lasting color.

Morphing - Firing

Helen Keller, deaf and blind American author, lecturer and activist, understood the necessity of risk-taking when she wrote, "Security is mostly a superstition. Avoiding danger is no safer in the long run than outright exposure. Life is either a daring adventure or nothing."

Most women step into the fire when they experience major life changes involving separation, such as retiring from a job, ending a difficult relationship, or sending their "babies" off to college. One might expect a sense of elation with these anticipated changes, but instead many of us feel cast adrift, lonely or abandoned. Because of our lack of connection or altered routines, our emotions fluctuate erratically. This emotional roller-coaster can be further intensified by the hormonal imbalances of menopause, another anticipated change that leaves many women feeling betrayed by their former younger bodies.

In the following sculpture, *Our Lady of Sorrow* (fig. 16 – following page), we see a shrouded, hollow, ghost-like figure. She has no face, no self-identity, and where she was once pregnant with life, she now carries emptiness in the pit of her stomach. The universe that use to surround her now rotates at her side, as she feels apart from the world of her past. What use to define her existence and provide a sense of purpose, now feels more like a ball and chain that she must drag along beside her.

During this period of detachment, many of us experience profound grief and sorrow for all that we perceive to have lost – our youth, our purpose or our goals. We may feel empty and confused when we look in a mirror and not recognize the face staring back at us. Although we continue to go through the motions of our old life, we feel like a stranger in a familiar land. We have entered a stage of mourning for the death of our dreams.

What most of us cannot comprehend at this juncture is how necessary and important it is for us to express our grief. Holding on to the regrets of our past can drain us of energy and make it impossible to live fully in the present. Research indicates that people who don't work through and release their emotions suffer decreased immune function, increased heart disease and susceptibility to illness. Grief, tears and sorrow are a natural part of the healing process during this challenging time of transformation.

When we learn to accept these changes not as losses, but as new opportunities for growth, we can fuel the energy of sadness into other creative outlets for physical and emotional healing. At the start of my own cocooning phase, a long and intense relationship ended with an intimate partner, followed shortly thereafter by a complete hysterectomy. Feeling both emotionally and physically hollow, I funneled my expressions of extreme loss into sculpting clay. This marked the beginning of the most artistically productive period of my life, and without sorrow serving as the catalyst, I might never have discovered this true manifestation of my inner self. This is for many of us the most creative time of our lives.

Ivy Baker Priest, first woman U.S. Treasurer, expressed this lemonade-from-lemons attitude in her following words, "The world is round and the place which may seem like the end may also be the beginning."

The Age of Cocooning

Fig. 16 – Our Lady of Sorrow

In the next sculpture, *Cloak of the Unknown* (fig. 17 – following page), we see a crouching figure wrapped in a shawl of black. Her staring eyes are sightless for she is incapable of seeing what lies ahead. Held captive within the blanketing cloak of fear, she still clutches her old belief systems tightly around herself for protection from the unknown. Since she isn't ready to express her new truths yet, and is afraid of their consequences, she covers her mouth to suppress her unspoken words.

Fig. 17 – Cloak of the Unknown

The Age of Cocooning

Despite her defensive posture, one naked foot emerges tentatively from beneath the cloak's protection. It is difficult to tell whether she is going to lunge forward into her future or fall back into her past. Instead she remains motionless, frozen by her fear. When many of us have spent our lifetimes defining ourselves through our attachments, we ask how do we now stand up for ourselves, speak our truths, and walk alone through this fire of transformation.

It is perfectly natural to feel afraid when we enter uncharted territory, because our survival mind (ego) only functions within the boundaries of the known. It thinks that since we survived before, we need to be cautious, calculating, and not do anything differently. Change computes as dangerous on our mind's computer, resulting in fearful resistance to new ideas or behaviors, even if they are ultimately for our own good.

Eleanor Roosevelt, American diplomat, humanitarian, and wife of President Franklin D. Roosevelt, understood this dilemma. She wrote in her memoirs, "You gain strength, courage, and confidence by every experience in which you really stop to look fear in the face. You *must* do the thing which you think you cannot do."

Taking this leap into the unknown can happen only when we are ready and willing to do so. To be *ready* usually happens when we have experienced enough pain to believe there is a greater possibility for pleasure through change than by staying the same. Being *willing* refers to having the courage to face deeper subconscious feelings and the awareness to change the beliefs that have caused these hardships. Usually, this involves facing dark aspects of our past.

Dr. Carl Jung, one of the 20th century's most influential psychological theorists, called this dark or negative side of our personality the "shadow." The shadow is composed of the tendencies, desires or actions we have perceived as embarrassing, dangerous, inferior or "bad," parts of ourselves we have tried to deny or repress. Although most of us don't wish to be identified with our shadow, our dark side is actually MORE damaging if we haven't recognized, owned, and incorporated it into our growing consciousness.

An integral part of accepting our shadow is our willingness to re-evaluate our ego states, the personalities that we wear for the rest of the world to see. These personas or masks are multi-faceted and may include dual roles. Conflicting personality traits such as doting mother and her shadow counterpart, the martyr; dedicated professional and its shadow, the workaholic; or compassionate friend, and its extreme, the doormat, can all be parts in our role repertoire. In order for us to evolve, these roles need to be examined and refashioned before we choose to put some of them back on.

As Women's Lib founder Gloria Steinem once said, "If the shoe doesn't fit, must we change the foot?" The answer is clearly "No," but if we truly want to transform, a willingness to change our footwear is our next step.

Although we will never lose our old ego states completely, through conscious awareness we can learn to accept them and choose new beliefs and behaviors that more closely align with our emerging truths. Dr. Jung called this struggle to become the Authentic Self the process of "individuation." This ongoing process will take a lifetime of self-evaluation and a willingness to change.

Morphing - Firing

In the following photo, *Wrapped Up in Myself* (fig. 18 – below), we see a phallic-like figure standing tall, alone, and surrounded by her cocoon of self-absorption. Her features are purposely evasive, since her true identity is yet undefined. Although she feels the uncertainty of where she may be headed, she trusts in her need to withdraw into herself.

Fig. 18 – Wrapped Up in Myself

Despite her motionless isolation, we can see the Kundalini (life-force) energy rising in dark blue spirals up from the statue's base. Unknown to those of us undergoing this period of deep self-reflection, powerful yin and yang energies are uniting within us, creating a balance and harmony we had been lacking before.

Yang energy, as mentioned before, is considered masculine in character. It is described as light, dry, directed, focused, logical, protective and action-oriented. Yin energy is viewed as feminine and is dark, moist, diffuse, vague, intuitive, emotional, nurturing and receptive. Most individuals identify with their birth gender energy in the first half of life, but in later years, many of us are drawn to integrate the opposite energy in a move toward wholeness.

In simplistic terms, at mid-life, men often begin to develop more capacity for relationship and experience greater emotional vulnerability. Women, however, may become more directive and assertive, and in the process, start to claim their independence, courage, and power. This phenomenon is what Gail Sheehy refers to in her book, *Passages*, as the "switch forties." This marks a significant shift away from the old dictates of cultural stereotyping and into a more authentic form of individuation.

In Summary

Like the caterpillar that spins a chrysalis around herself unaware of the great changes waiting within, most women enter the Age of Cocooning with a lack of clarity, direction or certainty. This is a period of profound personal metamorphosis marked by mounting feelings of loss, confusion and fear. We may feel uncomfortable in our own skin, as though our old life has become a too-tight garment that we have outgrown.

A rising restlessness causes us to question many aspects of our present existence and turn us away from the familiar. Although we feel big changes coming, we don't know the whys, the whens or the wherefores. We have entered a tight, dark space with no apparent way out and, for some of us, the pain of this uncertainty is more than we can handle.

Although they are dissatisfied with their current situation and crave change, for many women entering the darkness of the cocoon is too big a risk. Instead of confronting the dark or negative side of their personality – the shadow - these women will rationalize, deny, or swallow their truth in order to keep their status quo. Although they may be miserable, they are familiar with the face of their misery.

However, possibilities always exist for change.

Morphing - Firing

If we can honor and listen to the whisperings that call for our transformation, we will realize that our pain has a purpose. It heralds and accompanies growth, and presents us with life-altering experiences that offer valuable lessons to be learned. When we trust in the process and accept this period of withdrawal and self-reflection, the birthing of our Authentic Self can begin.

While positive new thoughts, beliefs, and behaviors are being adopted for change, other negative ones are also being released. For example, once confidence appears, we remove self-doubt. Once joy emerges, we let go of anger, and once acceptance abounds, we eliminate self-loathing.

It is interesting to note that if the chrysalis is pried open before the pupa is ready to come out, the butterfly will never develop and will die. Similarly, if the sculpture is taken out of the kiln too soon, the piece will be ruined. As a psychotherapist, I see this period for women as a time ripe for professional guidance. An understanding therapist can ease her client through the challenges more quickly while providing needed support.

If counseling is not possible, however, I recommend that each woman create a personal space, cocoon-like, where she can turn down the volume of the outside world. In this sanctuary, she may wish to include a small altar with a photo of herself as a young girl, the powerless inner child, who needs love and nurturing. Perhaps a flower, candle, incense, or journal can help honor and sanctify this place of healing. In this quiet space, we can practice and learn the art of Wise Woman mothering of ourselves.

It is heartening to know that once begun, the journey of self-actualization ususally is not reversible. Looking back, we will discover that the rewards gained from enduring these difficult times were worth the growing pains along the way.

Self-Help Worksheet
Stage Three: Morphing - *Firing*

Having completed your reading of Stage Three, it is *your* turn to respond to the artwork. Review each sculpture and allow your own thoughts and sensations to come foward. Written self-expression is a valuable tool in gaining deeper personal insight, so take your time in responding to the following questions. Use a separate sheet of paper for each photograph if needed.

Remember, your first impressions are often the most important ones and there are no right answers!

SELF-HELP EXERCISE:

What would you name this piece if you were the sculptor?

_____
_____
_____
_____
_____
_____
_____

What feelings, sensations or emotions does this piece evoke in you?

_____
_____
_____
_____
_____
_____
_____

Morphing - Firing

What scenes or memories from your life does this piece help you recall?

_____
_____
_____
_____
_____
_____

What thoughts or beliefs about your life come to mind while looking at this piece?

_____
_____
_____
_____
_____

If you don't like it, why not?

_____
_____
_____
_____

If you do like it, why?

_____
_____
_____
_____
_____

Four A's
Self-Help Worksheet
Stage Three: Morphing - *Firing*

Once again, please reflect upon what you may have learned about yourself from these excercises. It is now your chance to put this new awareness into action. Take all the time you need to answer the following questions thoughtfully and *honestly*. Use separate sheets of paper, if necessary.

1. AWARENESS

What negative beliefs about yourself have you held onto from this Morphing stage of your life? (Example: *"I am afraid to be alone."*)

_____
_____
_____
_____
_____
_____

What positive beliefs about yourself do you have from this Firing stage?

(Example: *"I trust my intuition, my inner voice."*)

_____
_____
_____
_____
_____
_____

2. ACCEPTANCE

What are you willing to accept as "authentic" beliefs about yourself after gaining this awareness?

_____
_____
_____
_____
_____
_____

3. ACTION

What old or dysfunctional beliefs and feelings are you willing to release about yourself?

_____
_____
_____
_____
_____
_____

What negative behaviors and habits are you willing to let go of?

_____
_____
_____
_____
_____
_____

4. APPRECIATION

Make a Gratitude List of the things you appreciate about yourself from this stage.

_____
_____
_____
_____
_____
_____
_____

What new beliefs have you fired into your mind from this list?

_____
_____
_____
_____
_____
_____
_____

What new behaviors will you embrace after emerging from the fire of transformation?

_____
_____
_____
_____
_____
_____
_____

Stage Four

Maturing - *Finishing*

Chapter Seven

The Age of Breakthrough

> "After a time of darkness comes the turning point. The old is discarded and
> the new appears. Persevere quietly on the path of inner truth.
> Return to the light in yourself … All is well."
> *Yi Jing, Chinese Oracle, 1150 BCE*

As we emerge from the confines of our cocoons, we sense that a major renewal has taken place within us. Our established ways of being and thinking have faded and a new reality awaits our creative self-expression. This liberation has freed our potential to develop our own unique authenticity. What were fantasies in our past are becoming the realities of our present.

Although this age of breakthrough seems to change the shape of everything, we do not leave our learnings of the past behind. Instead, we mold these lessons into new ways of thinking, such as the beliefs "everything happens for a reason," or "the problems of the past provide lessons for our highest good." This reframed mindset gives us the strength to move forward in gratitude, released from the doubt, anger and fear that had once encased us.

During the finishing stage in clay making, the kiln door is opened and the fired piece is taken out. It has lost as much as 12% of its original volume, making the pottery stronger, more resilient and more scratch-resistant than before. The glaze has fused with the clay beneath it, creating a vessel impervious to leaks and less likely to be affected by external pressures.

When the sculptor removes her piece from the kiln, however, she must be prepared for the unexpected changes that may have taken place during the firing. The piece may have cracked, the glaze may have darkened or run, and her creation may bear little resemblance to the one she envisioned before it entered the fire.

The same may be true for women at this finishing age of breakthrough. We must be prepared to examine who we really are and own all of our "cracks" and limitations, as well as our strengths and potentials.

In the following sculpture, *Letting Go* (fig. 19 – next page), we see a woman releasing the baggage from her past, as well as her expectations for the future. Her outstretched arms form a figure 8, the symbol of cyclical continuity, or eternity. She has no hands or fingers, as she is no longer grasping for things or people outside of herself. Instead, her arms are open-ended, allowing old beliefs to flow out of her and new truths to enter. Nor is she relying solely on input from without, but developing authenticity from within. Writer Gail Sheehy recognized this when she said, "Change is the essence of life. Be willing to surrender what you are for what you could become."

Fig. 19 – Letting Go

Although all of this sounds good on paper, some of you may be wondering how this applies to real life. How can we still formulate plans for ourselves without expectations? Isn't envisioning how we would like things to turn out an essential part of planning? The answer comes from the burgeoning Wise Woman within us. We do need our visions, plans, and action steps to thrive; however, we also must be willing to release our attachment to their outcome.

The journey of transformation is not a straight road, but a long and winding path. We often run into detours that take us off our chosen course, reminding us that change and balance require continual self-observation and evaluation. It isn't about achieving the goals; it is about taking the time to listen to our authentic voice and honor its truth.

The Age of Breakthrough

In the next sculpture, *The Light is Within* (fig. 20 – below), we see a seated woman with her head bent in contemplation. Her folded arms rest upon her knees, forming a circle around a candle lit from within. Her body has formed a quiet sanctuary protecting her from the outside world as she looks inside for self-illumination and guidance.

Fig. 20 – The Light is Within

It is said that prayer is asking and meditation is listening, so we need to be silent, open and receptive in order to hear the words of our true Authentic Self. Many people believe that we are sparks connected to the divine light of a higher consciousness, and only through the quiet will we be able to tap into this Source. Others think that the Source lies within and only through conscious awareness and clarity of intent, can we hear the whisperings of our inner Wise Woman. No matter how we tap into our Source, it is important that this quiet self-reflection be practiced on a regular basis, not just in times of stress or confusion.

Maturing - Finishing

The process of integrating our reality with our fantasies through conscious awareness usually starts for most women when they reach their forties. At this time, we begin to make life choices that serve our highest good, regardless of what others may think or want. As the pop singer Cher said, "I've always taken risks and never worried what the world might really think of me. I only answer to two people, myself and God."

This may sound selfish in a cultural context, but it has nothing to do with selfishness. This is not about taking from others, but about giving to our true Authentic Self. We can no longer hide or deny our emerging identity and are willing to take risks to honor it.

Fig. 21 – Mothering Herself

The Age of Breakthrough

This marks the beginning of conscious Self-care when we assume responsibility for our own needs and happiness. Although we can still be kind, generous, thoughtful and helpful to others, we have learned to temper our extremes of giving. Turn back to the sculpture *Anything to Please* on page 48 for a striking comparison between a self-sacrificing giver and a self-nurturing giver, as in the sculpture, *Mothering Herself* (fig. 21 – preceeding page).

In this piece, we see a curvaceous female form covered with multiple breasts. Her head rests contentedly on her left shoulder, which resembles the shape of an infant (her inner child) cradled lovingly within her arms. Unlike the figure in a previous sculpture, *Our Lady of Perpetual Giving* (page 52), whose breasts served the needs of others, this woman reserves her life-giving sustenance for herself first. If her milk should leak, it will be contained in the cup of her arm and conserved for her own growth and well-being.

By recognizing that self-nurturing behaviors feed us – whether they are sculpting, exercising, bubble baths, or journalling – we can mother ourselves by simply doing them. Whether we have a partner or not, whether our investments succeed or fail, or whether or not we can still run a marathon, our self-worth remains unaffected. Our personal worth can blossom independently from the external world.

In Summary

Having emerged transformed from the cocoon, women enter the Age of Breakthrough ready to cast off the burdens of their former selves and start anew. We have re-birthed ourselves and entered the infancy of a non-judgmental consciousness. This is a period marked by creative self-expression and reinvention. The fantasies of our past are quickly becoming the possibilities of our present, and we are learning to accept all of life's outcomes with equanimity. During this phase, contentment replaces resentment, composure supplants confusion and we grow to accept, not reject our realities.

Individualization and self-nurturing are also fostered and achieved at this stage of Maturing. Through conscious awareness, we have grown to value and honor the messages of our Authentic Self and express her truths. We also acknowledge the needs and desires of our inner child, and instead of turning to others to satisfy her endless desires, we learn to maturely mother ourselves. Without doing this self nurturing, we run the risk of being caught in destructive cycles again, trapping us in the past instead of moving us forward.

However, possibilities always exist for change.

Maturing - Finishing

In order to accomplish this major re-invention of ourselves, it is necessary to set aside time each day for quiet introspection. It is through continual self-reflection that we can develop a more objective observer's eye of our life. Since we now realize that we create our own experience through our thoughts and perceptions, we need to step outside of the hustle-bustle of our busy lives to nurture this self-awareness.

If we make the time to be in the moment, breathe in our new beliefs, while exhaling old, toxic ones, we can connect with our inner world of knowing and authenticity. We will be setting the stage to enter the Age of Truth with our eyes wide open and our mind/body/spirit poised to unite in a powerful connection unrealized before.

Chapter Eight

The Age of Truth

*"When I can look in the eyes, grown calm and wise, life will
have given me the Truth, and taken in exchange, my youth."*
Sara Teasdale, early 20th Century American Poet

During the Age of Truth, our growing awareness demands clarity and consciousness about our intentions. It is no longer just enough to face our truths; we must also be clear about what we want to do with them.

Although there is a developing Wise Woman within us during this phase of transformation, we still have our scared inner child and our belligerent teenager persona, as well. By becoming the Mother of this inner child/teenager, we need to accept the dual responsibility of both nurturing and disciplining her. As you can see in the previous sculpture, *Mothering Herself* (page 90), a strong, clearly defined black box (yang/discipline) surrounds the gentle, flowing mother figure (yin/yielding). In order to mother effectively, we need to balance both of these qualities and abilities.

This co-mingling of the yin and the yang is explored further in the next piece, *Head in Her Heart* (fig. 22 – page 94). At many times, our head – the logical and intellectual side of us – believes that it needs to run the show. It prompts us to take action and then evaluate the results from a purely analytical perspective.

For example, the head might say, "I should stay in the family business because I know it well and I make a lot of money." If the heart could speak, however, it might reply, "I really want to follow my passion of becoming an interior designer."

In this sculpture, we see the figure's head (logic) bent back into the heart space (feelings). The rational mind can now listen to the prompting of her intuition and emotion. When the mind and heart work together, reason becomes married to sentiment, and passion entwines with intellect. Yin and yang blend to create a more harmonious balance within the individual. The previous life choice dilemma could be resolved with a head/heart decision such as, "I will work part-time at my family's business and also go to art school part-time to earn a degree in design."

In order to achieve balance and harmony in a world of duality, the Wise Woman learns to integrate attributes and qualities from both sides. The path of balance between the two is narrow and requires constant adjustment to stay on course. We will continue to sway between these

Maturing - Finishing

dualities, but the Wise Woman at this age more quickly realizes when she is off-center and with willfulness returns to her place of balance. The chart on page 95, based on feng shui principles, may help you visualize this dynamic interplay of energies.

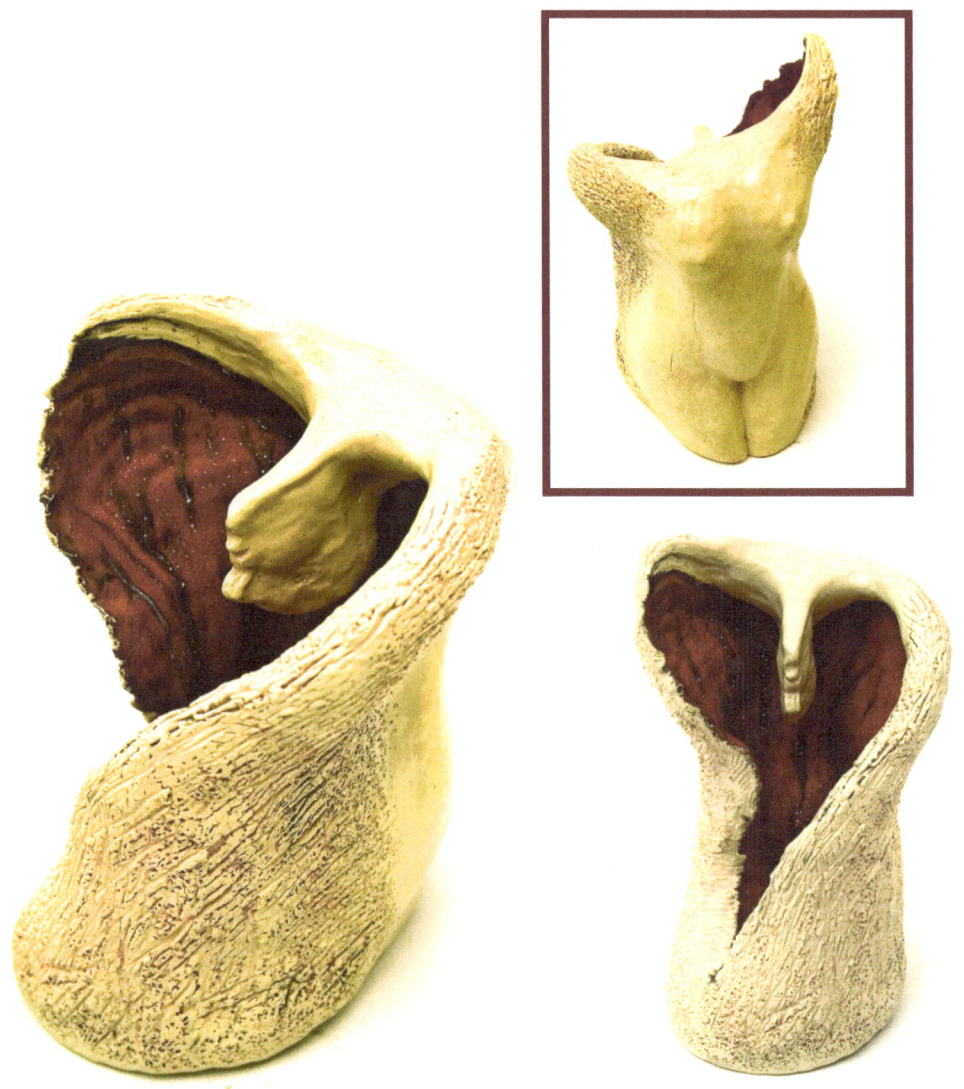

Fig. 22 – Head in Her Heart

As we move through this Age of Truth, it is also important to honor both the light and dark (shadow) sides of our psyche. The Wise Woman recognizes both the constructive and destructive elements of her being, and accepts both forces as she transforms. This dual dynamic energy is represented through the Hindu Goddess, Shakti, and the Hindu God, Shiva. Shakti signifies the fundamental creative force, and Shiva embodies destruction. Since it is our aim to become consciously balanced, the Wise Woman accepts both the Shakti and Shiva within herself. She honors the part that creates, as well as the side of her that destroys. Without destruction, there can be no new growth.

The Age of Truth

This duality, once accepted and integrated, can open up creative energies previously blocked to us. For some women, this balanced awareness may express itself through the creative arts, inventive cooking, gardening, further education or exotic travel. For others, it may be expressed through new ways of being in relationship or out-of-the-box thinking about work. No matter how it finds expression, this can be the most creative and growth-filled phase in a woman's life.

MASCULINE ENERGY	BALANCED	FEMININE ENERGY
Full	B	Empty
Outward	A	Inward
Hard	L	Soft
Contracted	A	Relaxed
Dry (rigid)	N	Wet (fluid)
Assertive	C	Passive
Protective	E	Nurturing
Penetrative	D	Receptive
Logical		Emotional
Light		Dark

Although we have made great strides towards re-inventing ourselves during the Age of Truth, our consciousness is still new and vulnerable to the pull of the past and the pressures of the present. In the following sculpture, *Centurion of Consciousness* (fig. 23 – following page), we see a female form clad in a suit of bronzed armor. Her warrior's sheath has breasts both front and back since she constantly must be vigilant in protecting her budding Authentic Self. Dangers lie ahead of her from without (the opinions and demands of others), and lurk behind her as well (the shouts of her Inner Child, Inner Teen and Inner Critic with the lure of their programmed beliefs).

In this piece, we also see a row of six colorful buttons running up the sides of the vestment, with a larger purple button nestled within the statue's top. Each button symbolizes one of the seven chakras of the Kundalini energy philosophy. Since I use this concept in many of my pieces, I'll briefly explain the theory. In yogic science, dating back nearly five millennia, chakras (or "disks of energy" in Sanskrit), were viewed as the body's intuitive or psychic energy system. Running up the center of the body along the spine, each chakra corresponds to a specific bodily function and is said to generate a particular form of energy or drive. This concept of chakras helps to explain the flow and integration of energies moving toward a higher consciousness.

The first chakra is said to rest at the base of the spine and its drive is toward security, survival, and the acquisition of material things. The Kundalini, or Serpent Power, is believed to lie sleeping here, ready to uncoil. This center, located near the anus, is associated with the bodily function of elimination, and is represented by the color red.

Maturing - Finishing

The second chakra is located in the genital area and is said to generate emotions, sexuality and creativity. This chakra corresponds to sex hormones involved in the reproductive cycle, which can cause dramatic mood swings, and is associated with the color orange.

Next comes the solar plexus chakra relating to assimilation and digestion. This chakra, found behind the navel, is linked to issues of power and is symbolized by the color yellow.

Fig. 23 – Centurion of Consciousness

The fourth or heart chakra is considered the energy source for our loving, intimate connections. This center, resting near the heart is said to control respiration, equilibrium, the immune system, and is green in color.

Our throat contains the fifth chakra driving our need for truthful communication and personal expression. This energy source is said to influence growth and maturation and is represented by the color blue.

The sixth chakra, also called the Third Eye, is stated to lie between the eyebrows where it generates intellect, and affects our consciousness, inner vision and light. This chakra is symbolized as the color indigo.

At the top of the head we find the seventh or Crown Chakra, believed to be the master chakra that controls all the others through the central nervous system. This energy source is often depicted just above the head as a halo, representing the physical basis of consciousness. This link to Divine energy is represented by a brilliant light with a purple glow.

Returning to the sculpture, *Centurion of Consciousness* (fig. 23-p.96), notice that the purple (crown chakra) button on the top left is larger than the rest. This implies that the woman has achieved, at this phase of her personal growth, a heightened spiritual connection to all things, to her Higher Self, and to Divine Energy. Her life force energy, like her new Observer-Mind Consciousness, requires vigilant care and protection to keep it aligned. As Buddha once said, "If you hold yourself dear, protect yourself well."

In the next piece, *Mind-Body* (fig. 24 –following page), we see the total integration of the mental and physical components within the figure. Unlike the previous sculpture, *Head in Her Heart* (page 94), in which the intellect and beliefs of the mind are intentionally filtered through the emotions and intuitions of the heart, here the blending of the two is nearly effortless. The mind-body marriage is complete and their connection is seamless.

In order to achieve our natural balance we must "mind" our body. Emotions and desires come to us as flowing sensations felt in the body, and we experience mental and physical tension when our minds create denial, avoidance and resistance to these feelings. By accepting the reality of what is, we release the stresses caused by this internal conflict.

To maintain our conscious awareness, it is important to ask the following questions:

- *What part of my body is feeling this conflict?*
- *What is the message in this sensation?*
- *How old is this belief/emotion?*
- *Is this feeling attached to a belief from my past which no longer serves me?*
  Or is this an insightful, intuitive directive of higher consciousness?

Maturing - Finishing

The Wise Woman's quest is to master the mind-body connection and decipher its messages. It takes conscious awareness to heal our old emotional wounds and beliefs, to ask and answer these difficult questions, and to recognize the prompting of our true Authentic Self.

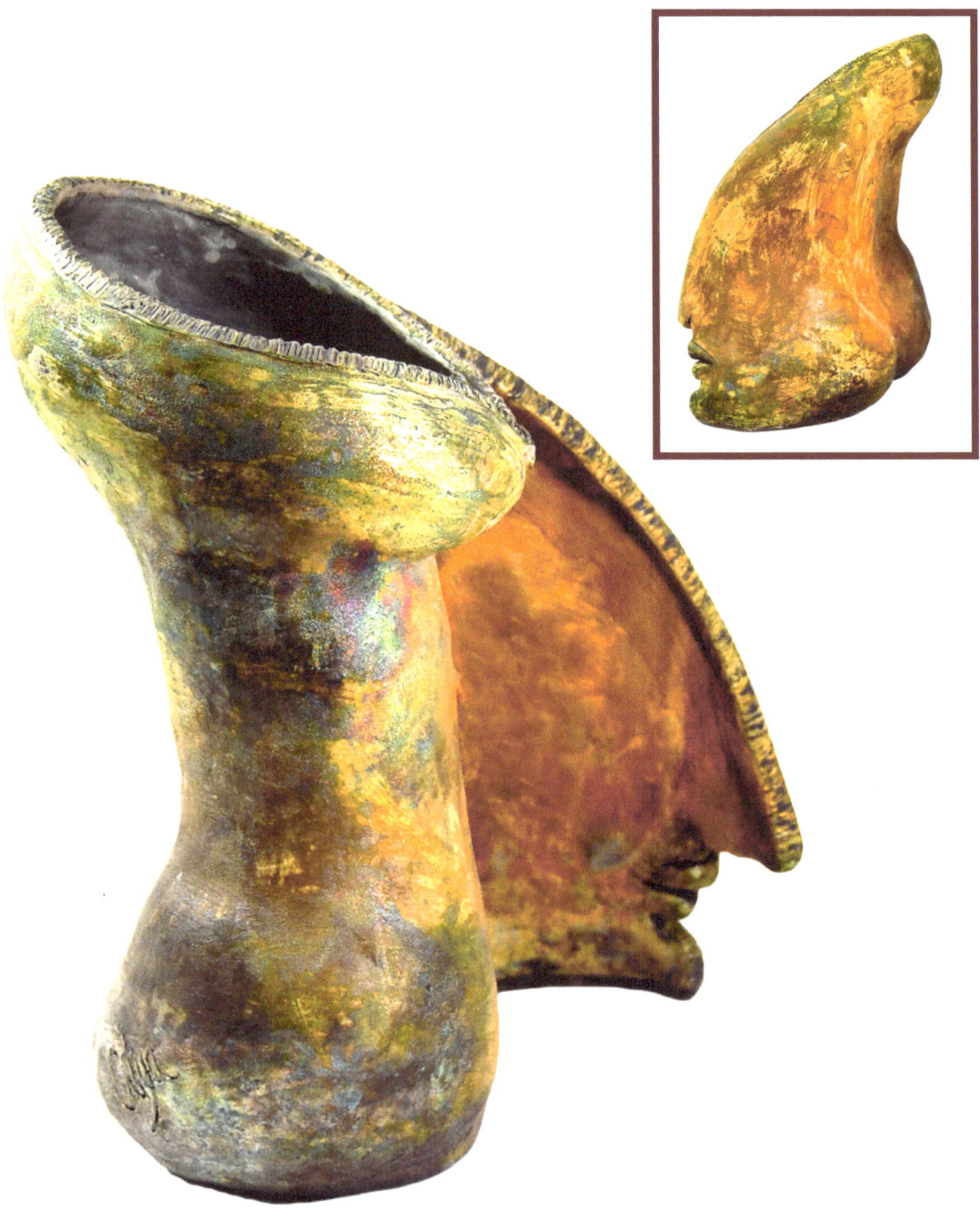

Fig. 24 – Mind-Body

In Summary

In our Age of Truth, we strive for conscious awareness and clarity of intention. We have reached a place of balance between our thinking minds and our feeling, intuitive hearts, between our yin and our yang, and have found a healthy compromise between our power to create anew and the need to release the old.

This process of integrating dualities is a necessary part of attaining wholeness of mind, body and spirit. If the yogic system of chakras is used to illustrate this, most people would appear to be stuck in the lower three chakras, which control behaviors of tribalism, sexuality and materialism. This limited perspective is rooted in fear and power which lacks the compassion, creative expression and spirituality available when we travel up into higher chakra energies. When all seven chakras are aligned and unified within the individual, it is said balance and consciousness flourish.

Walking the narrow path of balance is challenging for most of us and unsustainable for others. Our minds, programmed by old ways of being, require watchful vigilance for us to remain consciously aware. It is easy to fall back into familiar, yet destructive behavior patterns, especially when the people, places, and things around us provide triggers to our past. Although we have acknowledged our authentic truths, we still require an ongoing commitment to our personal growth to protect them.

However, possibilities always exist for change.

When we become conscious observers of our thoughts and actions, the Wise Woman within quickly realizes when we have lost our footing on the narrow path of balance. Instead of tumbling down the slippery slope to our past thinking and behaviors, we will regain equilibrium sooner and march with confidence into the Age of Acceptance that lies ahead.

Self-Help Worksheet
Stage Four: Maturing - *Finishing*

Turn back through the pages of Stage Four and review each of the sculptures. It is now *your* turn to respond to the artwork. Take your time in answering each of the following questions about any of the pieces that speak to you. Use additional sheets of paper, if necessary.

Remember, your first impressions are often the most important ones and there are no right answers!

SELF-HELP EXERCISE:

What would you name this piece if you were the sculptor?

_____
_____
_____
_____
_____
_____
_____

What feelings, sensations or emotions does this piece evoke in you?

_____
_____
_____
_____
_____
_____
_____

The Age of Truth

What scenes or memories from your life does this piece help you recall?

_____
_____
_____
_____
_____
_____

What thoughts or beliefs about your life come to mind while looking at this piece?

_____
_____
_____
_____
_____

If you don't like it, why not?

_____
_____
_____
_____
_____

If you do like it, why?

_____
_____
_____
_____
_____

Four A's
Self-Help Worksheet
Stage Four: Maturing - *Finishing*

Use the following exercises to help you express the new insights you have gained about yourself through this reading. Take all the time you need to answer the following questions thoughtfully and *honestly*. Use separate sheets of paper, if needed.

1. AWARENESS

What negative beliefs about yourself have you held onto from this Maturing stage of life? (Example: *"It's too hard for me to stay balanced."*)

_____
_____
_____
_____
_____
_____

What positive beliefs about yourself do you have from this Finishing stage? (Example: *"I can and will take good care of myself."*)

_____
_____
_____
_____
_____
_____

2. ACCEPTANCE

What are you willing to accept as authentic beliefs about yourself after gaining this awareness?

_____
_____
_____
_____
_____
_____

3. ACTION

What old or dysfunctional beliefs and feelings are you willing to release about yourself?

_____
_____
_____
_____
_____
_____

What negative behaviors and habits are you willing to let go of?

_____
_____
_____
_____
_____
_____

4. APPRECIATION

Make a Gratitude List of the things you appreciate about yourself from this stage.

___

What new beliefs have you integrated into your life from this list?

___

What new behaviors are you willing to embrace with this conscious awareness?

___

Stage Five

Matroning - *Freeing*

Chapter Nine

The Age of Acceptance

"The heyday of a woman's life is the shady side of fifty."
Elizabeth Cady Stanton, Women's Rights Activist (1815-1902)

The Random House Dictionary defines the word "matron" in the following ways:

1) A wife or a widow, especially one who has borne children.
2) A woman of staid or motherly manners with an established social position.
3) A housekeeper; especially a woman who manages the domestic economy of a public institution, such as head nurse in a hospital or an attendant, guard or warden in a school or facility.

I have chosen the term "Matroning" to refer to the stage in a woman's life when she has developed "staid and motherly manners" towards herself and to others. She has become the "housekeeper" who "manages the domestic economy" of her own life, where she, herself, is the "home." During this period of Matroning, we establish a new "social position," that of becoming our own mothers. This doesn't mean that we are turning into or mimicking the ones that birthed us, but we are transforming into the benevolent, yet disciplined Mother of our own Authentic Self.

By the time we reach this stage, most of us have entered a plateau of peaceful acceptance. Unlike previous periods of resignation, in which we gave up a hard-fought struggle after prolonged resistance, acceptance is a kinder, gentler form of acquiescence. During our lifetimes we are asked to accept many things - other people, our work, our obligations and responsibilities – but, at this age of personal growth, we give up our resistance to accepting our lives and ourselves as they really are.

Acceptance is the peaceful acknowledgement of what is, which opens the door to growth, change, gratitude and contentment. When we surrender to acceptance, we are finally free to "be."

During the freeing stage in ceramics, the potter has removed her piece from the kiln and is faced with the decision of how to best put it to use. If the piece is less than perfect, the artist may envision a different future for it than originally intended. The time has come for her truthful assessment. Will her vessel be a showpiece admired for its beauty alone, or be mainly utilitarian? Will her creation serve as a legacy to inspire, educate or instruct others, or will it end up in the corner of a cluttered closet?

Matroning - Freeing

No matter what she decides, the matron artist will make this choice freed from judgments about good or bad. She will simply look at her creation, taking in all of its imperfections as well as its assets, and remark, without shame or blame, "Hmmm...this is interesting! What have I learned and how shall I creatively proceed?"

Having passed through the Age of Truth, women now have reached an acceptance of their realities. In the following sculpture, *No Body's Perfect* (fig. 25 – below), we see a female form with many physical characteristics deemed as defects by our society. Her figure is small-breasted and bottom heavy, her thighs are large and dimpled with cellulite and age spots, and she bears the ragged edges of scars running up her sides.

Fig. 25 – No Body's Perfect

The Age of Acceptance

Despite all of these individual imperfections, when viewed as a whole, there is a flowing beauty about this piece. This sculpture lacks a head with a critical mind, thereby freeing the figure from the judgment of herself or others. This allows her to accept the worthiness of her whole being as is.

Prior to entering this Age of Acceptance, women are affected by the belief systems and constraints of our culture. We worry if we are thin enough, sexy enough, or rich enough. Our judgments have come from standards arbitrarily imposed upon us from without, but during this stage of transformation, the standards shift firmly to within. We are free to enjoy our own uniqueness.

From my own pubescence on, I waged a war of love/hate with my derriere. When I was a teenager, my mother would ask me, trying to be helpful, "You're not going to wear that, are you? It is such a shame your behind looks so big." Granted, my bottom has always been a size larger than my top, so I spent most of my life trying to hide my "imperfection."

It wasn't until I entered this radically accepting phase of Matroning that I finally quieted my Inner Critic. I have learned that perfection exists only in the dictionary, and have come to at least tolerate, if not embrace, all of my unique and ever-changing Stages. I now have the belief, "I am perfectly imperfect!" By changing our mindset, we open ourselves up to self-acceptance and by equating self-worth with self-improvement, we are free to grow and move forward.

Some of you may be asking yourselves, "Is acceptance of our perceived imperfections a requirement to personal growth? Will I be a lesser being if I still feel the need to color my hair or get Botox?" The answer to this dilemma can be answered with another question – for whom are you doing these things? Do you keep your hair a youthful shade of #10 chestnut brown because you fear no one will desire you with silver tresses? Or are you continuing your rendezvous with hair dye because you feel better? Is it about pleasing YOU or about pleasing others?

If you are striving to enhance your natural beauty because it makes you happier and more self-confident, then keep it up! Understanding who you are and what you need to do to take care of yourself is a form of acceptance. We can still be true to our inner self when our outer self is redecorated. It is all about intention and the motivations that prompt our alterations. Plato said, "Beauty lies within the eyes of the beholder" and we are the most important beholders of our own beauty within.

In the next sculpture, *Decorate Yourself* (fig. 26 – following page), we see a stooped crone dressed in a boldly decorated purple robe. She has a quizzical, yet intense look upon her wrinkled face as she peers out at the world with wonder and awe.

She has grown wise through surviving many life lessons, yet she appears to be seeing the world anew. By removing the blinders of her past conditioning and accepting herself unconditionally – wear and tear included – she no longer has to live in any particular way. She doesn't mind if the color purple is in style, or if the wild designs on her back are pleasing to others. She has made the choice to wear them boldly because they suit her.

Matroning - Freeing

Upon closer inspection, you will also notice that this sculpture can be viewed in more ways. She is a matronly woman with pendulous breasts when seen from the front, but she resembles an erect penis and scrotum when turned to the side. This duality suggests that women, at this stage of transformation, have integrated both their feminine and masculine aspects and are equally receptive and assertive.

Despite the freedom that most of us feel when we move into acceptance, this transition also requires a good deal of courage. It is not easy walking the narrow path of balance alone towards our goals knowing that trust may be our only means of support. As the American actress and author Dorothy Bernard once said, "Courage is fear that has said its prayers."

Fig. 26 – Decorate Herself

In the following sculpture, *Courage* (fig. 27 – following page), we see a tattered angel who has been through life's fire. Unlike the angel in a previous work, *Hanging On* (page 53), who had collapsed face down in Mother Earth's mud, this angel came out the other side facing up with her wings widespread, ready to soar in heart, mind and spirit.

The Age of Acceptance

Although this female's body shows well-worn wounds of her journey, she has gained a spiritual wisdom that outlasts the transient beauty of the flesh. Her legs are crossed now for protection, unlike her younger self that lay spread-legged in *Hanging On*. Both angels are connected to Mother Earth, but in this sculpture, the matron is readying for flight again, receiving her strength from the "mother" within. This mature angel blends her earthiness with wisdom and trust, and cautiously protects her vulnerabilities from the violence of life.

This angel represents our inner warrior who has persevered through many fires and survived. With her naiveté burned away, she sets and maintains strong boundaries, has the strength to speak up assertively for her ideals, and provides a protective presence for others less developed.

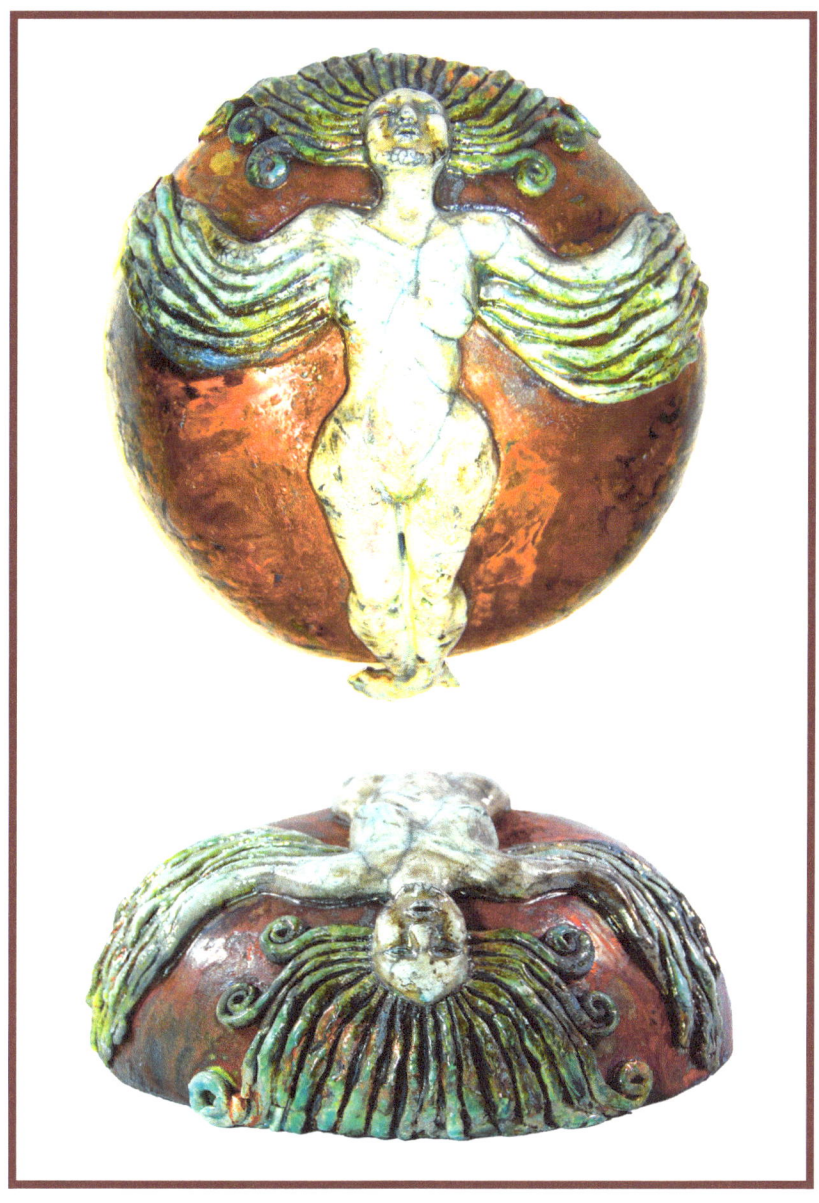

Fig. 27 – Courage

This concern for others less enlightened reflects our growing "self-less" compassion at this stage. We have less of our ego self at this time, yet our universal self is expanding. This heightened sense of empathy for all beings allows us to feel at one with everything. We continue to have preferences in life, but we now realize that our former judgments were divisive and separating. We have learned to balance our personal preferences with what is best for the greater good.

Reaching this place of balance requires the difficult task of letting go, giving in, and giving up many of our resistances. Just as a kite must let go of resistance in order to dance in the buoyant currents of the wind, we too must release our historical echoes of fear and conditioning to dance with our desired destiny. Through acceptance and gratitude, we become like kite strings attached to both a grounded authentic knower within and an elevated transcendent truth from without. The freedom we gain is well worth the effort necessary to obtain it.

In Summary

By the time we enter the first phase of Matroning, most of us have reached an internal place of peaceful acceptance. Our resistance has diminished into embracing our lives and ourselves as we really are, and we have become the loving, yet disciplined " mothers" of our Authentic Self.

Much of the contentment gained at this stage of transformation comes from the silencing of our harsh inner critic. We have learned to accept our imperfections along with our attributes without making judgments of good or bad. This lack of self-criticism, blame and shame frees us to rejoice in our own uniqueness. The doors open wide to creative self-expression and despite the hard lessons learned, the world can appear anew, fresh with possibility.

Freeing the Authentic Self can be liberating, but also frustrating when our outer shells – our bodies – have become tattered by time. Despite the freedoms gained through our unconditional self-acceptance, many of us have limited options due to our creeping aches and pains or challenging health conditions.

However, possibilities always exist for change.

Although our bodies may move more slowly than before, our hearts, minds and spirits are unencumbered, allowing us to soar more effortlessly than in younger years. We have reached a place of balance that unites many of the dualities that divided us before. Our inner strengths allow us to walk the narrow path of balance with little fear, and although we may be alone, we have trust as our allied companion. We have tapped into a higher state of conscious awareness and self-reliance, and the Wise Woman is emerging in all of her glory.

Chapter Ten

The Age of Wisdom

"Never mistake knowledge for wisdom. One helps you make a living; the other helps you make a life."
Sandra Carey, Author

During the Age of Wisdom, we have acknowledged, accepted and integrated all of the roles we have played throughout our lifetime into a single wholeness of being. As we reflect back upon the stages of our personal transformation, we realize that they have all been necessary steps to bring us to this place of oneness. Our masculine and feminine energies are in balance and we feel connected to both our Source and to all people and things.

The Wise Woman emerges when she combines knowledge with experience to reveal the meaning behind her life's journey. By recognizing the unique gifts she brings to the world, the Wise Woman can define her life's purpose, strive to make it manifest, and help others find theirs. Regardless of what a particular day may bring, be it pain or pleasure, her purpose for being alive remains steady. Her body may have lost its strength or elasticity, but she has gained flexibility of will and the power of her conscious awareness.

Just as the artist understands the series of steps and processes that build upon one another to create a finished work of art, the Wise Woman also recognizes that she builds upon a lifetime of conscious choices to create a strong inner foundation. The clay of her being has hardened at this point and instead of having to sell or display her greatest work of art – herself – she is living it. She no longer questions what she can produce at this stage of transformation, but concentrates on what she has become. She is one with the clay, with her body-mind-heart.

To reach this place of total integration, the Wise Woman must first recognize, honor and fully accept all of her parts as is. In the following sculpture, *Feminine Landscape* (fig. 28 – p. 114), we see a partial female figure covered with many of the characters she has been in her past – the powerless Inner Child, the rebellious Inner Teen, the unrelenting Inner Critic, as well as the Inner Angel of Courage. All of these personalities still live within her, yet she no longer identifies with just one of these roles since she is more than a combination of them all. She has become the compassionate but disciplined director of her multi-faceted cast of characters – the fearful Inner Child, the defiant Inner Teen, and the ruthless Inner Critic - and no longer allows them to run her show. She has given herself permission to be all of these less-than-perfect selves, because they are all a necessary part of the human condition.

Matroning - Freeing

Despite all of the scars, stitches and bulges life has inflicted upon this figure, there is a flowing beauty and grace about the piece. Her hips and breast bear deep gashes or wounds, yet these serve as medals of honor for a life lived with fortitude. By her widespread stance we can tell that this woman is moving forward in full stride and no matter what life may throw in her way, she will continue on her path with conscious conviction.

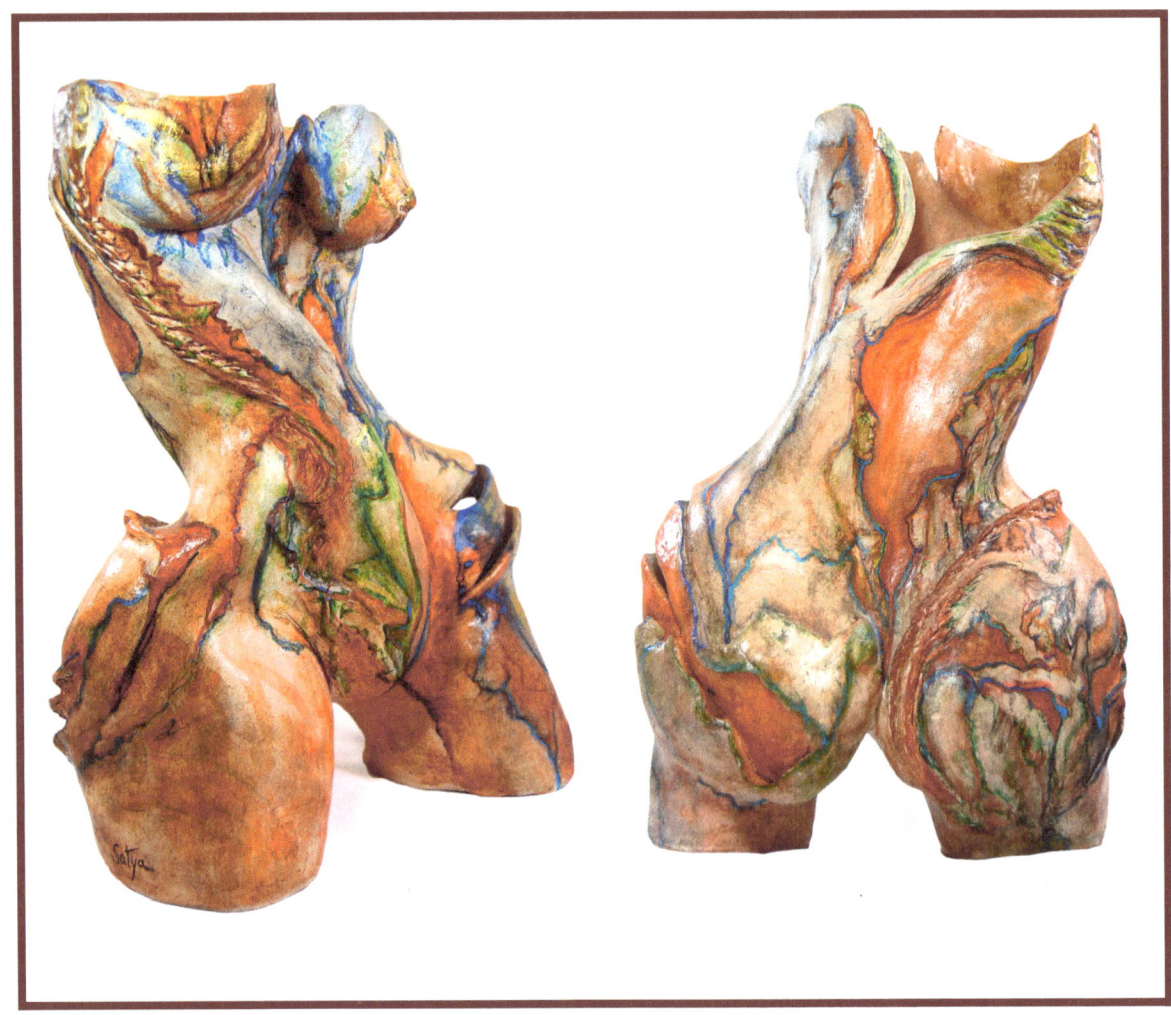

Fig. 28 – Feminine Landscape

Like most of my other pieces, this work is an open vessel, in this case symbolizing the figure's receptivity to the light of her Higher Consciousness. Lacking a head, her specific identity is insignificant, since she represents all women at this stage of transformation who search for a consciousness far greater than that of their ego.

Despite her growing wisdom, the older woman in our society is not given the same respect or appreciation she has garnered in other parts of the world. In the United States, she is often overlooked and undervalued compared to the more productive youthful members of her gender.

The Age of Wisdom

In the next sculpture, *Kneeling Crone* (fig. 29 – below), we see a woman leaning on a pedestal as if in prayer. Her eyes are closed as she looks within herself for guidance. She has seen most of what the world can offer her and has integrated the life lessons it has taught. Although her right foot is still firmly planted on the world, what matters most to her now is the voice of her own Authentic Self.

Although advanced in years, this figure remains strong as she kneels reverently at the Temple of the Masculine. Unlike the earlier sculpture, *Cocksure* (page 35), where the smug maiden sits on top the pedestal of masculinity believing she is above it, the elderly crone has learned to respect the yang energy within and honors its power. Her strength now comes from within, while the maiden's strength was borrowed from without.

Fig. 29 – Kneeling Crone

Take a second glance at this sculpture and you will notice that the crone is caressing the long snake draped beside her. This action symbolizes the peaceful integration of the woman with change and the continuing cycles of transformation. Like the snake that must shed her skin in order to grow, the Wise Woman recognizes that this process of rebirth is never-ending.

Matroning - Freeing

Both of these sculptures were purposefully left unglazed, because each figure is still in a state of incompletion. The maiden is just beginning her journey and has much to learn before she is finished, while the crone is wise enough to know that we are never finished.

At this stage of Matroning, many women find themselves living alone, whether it is by choice or by happenstance. Unlike a younger woman who may be terrified by the prospect of a single existence, the Wise Woman has learned to release her fears about being alone. She has befriended the many characters she has adopted in her lifetime and turns within to share their memories, stories, lessons and experiences. Instead of feeling "alone," she understands that she is "all-one" within herself and with all beings. The Wise Woman has become her own best companion.

Many single women at this age consider this period to be one of the most gratifying times of their life. They may feel connected to their communities through their volunteerism, to their families and friends through their shared experiences, to the greater world around them through their wisdom, and most importantly, they feel connected to themselves.

Thriving within oneself is a question of balance. Those of us who have had to multi-task throughout our lives – handling responsibilities at home as well as in a career – are usually fine when left to our own devices. We are well prepared to handle our own emotional and practical needs. Those people, however, who have lived primarily one sided in either their yin or yang energy, will find it more challenging to thrive alone.

Contentment within oneself is not guaranteed for every woman at this stage of Matroning. If she had been in a long-term dependent relationship with a partner who did everything for her, such as paying the bills or driving the car, this woman may get sick or rapidly decline when left alone. She often lacks the necessary resourcefulness to find companionship within herself.

In the following pair of sculptures, *Standing Meditation* and *Sitting Meditation*, (figs. 30 and 31) we see two figures who have found their proper balance. Both are looking up to their Higher Consciousness and both have their hands opened to receive its messages and guidance. The life force energy in these women is focused now on their crown chakra of spiritual connection.

Their physical presence is still valued by these women (notice the shiny lean physique of the standing one and the colorful decorations on the one who is seated), but their awareness and attention is upward and within. It is not that they are preparing themselves to leave their bodies, but they have grasped the greater importance of their connection to their Source.

Both of these sculptures are containers with tops that come off to hold precious treasures inside. This symbolizes that our bodies have become sacred vessels to store the jewels of wisdom experience has brought us over the years. The body is no longer valued solely for its physicality, but as the earthly connection to the spirit within. We are spiritual beings having a human experience.

Even at this advanced stage of transformation, women are still in a state of continuous flux. I have used the metaphor of the empty vessel once again to symbolize that in all stages of growth we "leak," and it is our responsibility to renew, refresh and refill ourselves. We do this

The Age of Wisdom

through our ongoing commitment to personal growth and enlightenment. If we steadfastly align our beliefs and behaviors with our Wise Woman intentions, we become that open vessel capable of being endlessly refilled by higher consciousness.

Fig 31. - Sitting Meditation

Fig. 30 - Standing Meditation

Matroning - Freeing

Returning to the sculptures, you can see each of these pieces has a large, stable base representing our balanced foundation at this stage of personal evolution. All chakras are in alignment in these figures, as their mind-body-spirit connection grows ever stronger.

No matter what is happening in our everyday lives, by this stage of transformation we are continually open to our Higher Consciousness. Whether we are standing in line at the bank or sitting at home reading a book, we can connect to our Source. Unlike in previous stages where we needed to withdraw from our daily activities through meditation or yoga to reach that inner knowing, we now can live from that place of awareness.

There are some, however, who will never reach that inner wholeness no matter how long they live or how much they withdraw. Unless we have gone through the fire, we will stay grounded in the energies of the lower chakras and the egos that bind them. Those of us who have chosen the rigorous path of the Authentic Self can arrive at this plateau of unity and enlightenment.

Becoming the Wise Woman is not a natural process that just happens as a result of advancing age. She evolves instead from the willful choices made to gain conscious awareness during each stage of her lifetime. A Higher Consciousness can't be handed to us through a particular religion or through the teachings of someone else. It must be earned individually by making intentional decisions and doing the hard work of personal growth over the course of many years.

In the next sculpture, *Retiring* (fig. 32 –following page), we see a female figure with a flower for her head. Unlike the earlier piece, *Opening* (page 28), which showed a young girl as a bloom unfolding into life, here we see a flower who is past her prime. Although she is still lovely, she is starting to lean and no longer is the fragrant, colorful blossom that she was in her youth. Where once she was unfurling, she is now starting to close.

In her childhood, the girl required nurturing from without to survive, just as a flower needs sunlight and water to grow. At this stage, however, the woman's nurturing comes from the fullness within. Her petals have turned a bit brown around the edges and are folding inward for sustenance from within her core. She is now flowering in a different way by drawing from her own wisdom to give forth to the world.

At this stage, we have reached not only our apex of feminine receptivity, but have also integrated our masculine qualities as well. If you look at this piece from the one side, you will see a peaceful woman with an ample bosom, flowing gracefully down into her solid, matronly form. When viewed from the other, her bosom transforms into three flaccid penises draped down her side.

Although she contains both the yin and yang within her, these energies have entered a more passive stage. This doesn't imply that the woman is no longer of value, but that her presentation has changed. At this time, some of us may choose to mentor others, write books or teach as a form of giving back some of our wisdom. We are no longer driven by an ego-based quest for achievement or to take center stage. The Wise Woman has arrived at a place of restfulness and is gently folding back the petals to her life within.

The Age of Wisdom

Fig. 32 – Retiring

In Summary

The Age of Wisdom is a mystical and reflective time. We ponder the deeper meanings of life as we come to realize our grander purpose for being alive. After years of conscious cultivation, the Wise Woman has emerged to guide us with clarity and insight. We have grown to trust our instincts and to listen to the truth of our authentic voice.

Wisdom is something we cannot be taught or acquired as a natural outgrowth of aging. It is a state of being that evolves from a lifetime of making conscious choices to live in a willfully balanced way. Just as we can read about the attributes, sensations and expressions of love, until we have experienced it firsthand, they are only concepts. The same holds true for wisdom.

However, possibilities always exist for change.

Through the quietude that comes with wisdom, we are able to connect more deeply with others, the world around us and to our Higher Consciousness. Although we may have become less aggressive or showy at this age, we are still able to share our personal gifts and attributes in important, creative ways. The Wise Woman has fully united her yin and yang energies, although they are expressed with less bravado than before. We have reached a place of calm centeredness that paves the way to the Age of Completion.

Chapter Eleven

The Age of Completion

> "We should so provide for old age that it may have no urgent wants of this world to absorb it from meditation on the next."
> Pearl S. Buck, *winner of the Pultizer Prize and Nobel Prize for Literature*

As we enter the final stretch of our life's journey, we find ourselves wondering about not only what lies ahead, but also about what might lie *beyond* our earthly existence. In ancient times, this period was known as the age of initiation into the mysteries of life. Just as we sense our connection to our Source strengthening, we also feel our grip on earthly attachments loosening.

We have come a long way on our journey, often re-circling the same paths until we were ready to move on. Each time we crossed the threshold to a new stage, however, we were able to enter the unknown with a growing sense of wisdom and calm. We have become familiar with the quiet within us and welcome its presence as we turn down the volume on the outside world.

For most of us, this is a time of deep reflection – a time for looking back to measure the significance of our lifetime. A good question to ask is, "Did I enjoy the journey?" Better yet, "Was I conscious enough to trust and co-create with my Authentic Self?" After all, as a wise teacher of mine once said, "Happiness is not a destination; it is a way to travel."

When I think about this concept in terms of my art, I don't measure my success by how many pieces I have sold or how much I have liked each one of them, but by what I have learned along the way. I realize that my art, as my life, has been an unfolding process of continuous creation. It is this process of creative transformation itself that I have valued and enjoyed.

In writing this book, I have spoken from personal experience having walked through each of these stages up to this final one, Completion. I have only witnessed others going through it and their experiences have filled me with awe. For ten years, I took care of my ailing mother, a feisty, fiercely independent woman, who fought a losing battle against Alzheimer's disease. With this illness as her commander, I watched my mother gradually being forced to let go of everything in her life – even her ego – her identity. The following piece, *Completion* (fig. 33 – next page), was created to honor her profound experience with letting go.

Matroning - Freeing

Unlike all of my other works that are shaped from a solid piece of clay, this one is made of coils. The process of rolling out each coil and connecting it to the others is long and tedious, just as her life seemed to become long and tedious at this stage.

The figure in this work is a spiral coiling upward towards her Source. While her eyes close, her face rises, appearing to discern what comes next, Mother Earth is also calling her drooped and sagging body back home. She has become heavy from carrying the weight of her years and seems to be looking beyond for a release from her worldly burdens.

Fig. 33 – Completion

The Age of Completion

Just as the clay of her body is returning to the earth, this figure's mind has returned to a state of childlike naiveté. Her tiny head is representative of her shriveled ego-identity. I also carved a pure and simple heart over her heavy breasts to symbolize its full circle back to where it started. Once again, the heart has become an innocent and empty vessel waiting to be filled – once more.

This concept of the endless circle of life continues in this final piece, *It's All Clay* (fig. 34 – below). I was thinking of the biblical quote, "for dust thou art and unto dust shalt thou return" when I created this work. Here we see an open bowl with a rim encircled by the repetitious cycles of existence. An amorphous lump of clay becomes a snake (transformation), which morphs into an animal (the ego mind), which changes into a woman (physical reality), who transforms into a skeleton (death) in this ever-evolving continuum.

Fig. 34 – It's All Clay

It wasn't until I looked closely at the photograph taken of this piece, however, that I noticed the startling female face that appeared in the glaze at the bottom of the bowl (fig. 35 –below). In real life, this apparition is invisible – the glaze is dark and devoid of any image.

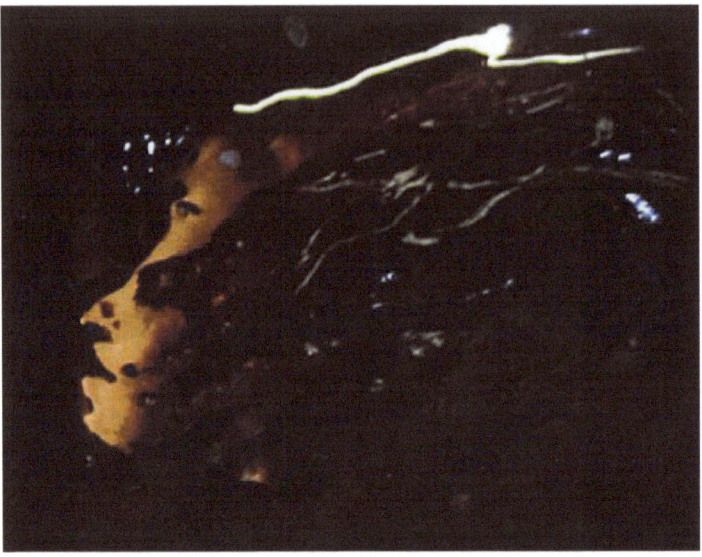

Fig. 35 – It's All Clay
(Close-up image of Spirit Woman)

In the photograph, however, this ephemeral "Spirit Woman," with a pronounced third eye, stares directly at the female figure on the edge of the bowl, almost as if they are in deep communion. I interpret this spectral image to mean that my Source, Spirit, Wise Woman, Devine Energy, Higher Consciousness – whatever you wish to call it – is watching over me; especially when I am in the dark, into the fire, or just unaware of her presence. I imagine she is telling me that I am not alone and that my journey is, after all, a process and my greatest work of art. It is my fervent belief that She is also there for you.

The Age of Completion

"Don't cry because it is over; smile because it happened." (unknown)

Self-Help Worksheet
Stage Five: Matroning - Freeing

Turn back through the pages of Stage Five and review each of the sculptures. It is now *your* turn to respond to the artwork. Take your time in answering the following questions about the pieces that speak to you. Use additional sheets of paper if needed.

Remember, your first impressions are often the most important ones and there are no right answers!

SELF-HELP EXERCISE:

What would you name this piece if you had created it?

_____
_____
_____
_____
_____
_____
_____

What feelings, sensations or emotions does this sculpture stir in you?

_____
_____
_____
_____
_____
_____
_____

The Age of Completion

What scenes or memories from your life does this piece help you recall?

_____
_____
_____
_____
_____

What thoughts or beliefs about your life come to mind while looking at this piece?

_____
_____
_____
_____
_____

    If you don't like it, why not?

_____
_____
_____
_____

    If you do like it, why?

_____
_____
_____
_____

Four A's
Self-Help Worksheet
Stage Five: Matroning - *Freeing*

Use the following exercises to help you express the new insights you have gained or may have learned about yourself through this reading. Take all the time you need to answer the following questions thoughtfully and *honestly*. Use separate sheets of paper, as needed.

1. AWARENESS

What negative beliefs about yourself have you held onto from this Matroning stage of your life? (Example: *"I am no longer attractive or useful."*)

_____
_____
_____
_____
_____
_____

What positive beliefs about yourself do you have from this Freeing stage?
(Example: *"I am grateful for all I have and all I have experienced."*)

_____
_____
_____
_____
_____
_____

2. ACCEPTANCE

What are you willing to accept as authentic beliefs about yourself after gaining this awareness?

_____
_____
_____
_____
_____
_____

3. ACTION

What old or dysfunctional beliefs and feelings are you willing to release about this stage?

_____
_____
_____
_____
_____
_____

What negative behaviors and habits are you willing to let go of?

_____
_____
_____
_____
_____
_____

4. APPRECIATION

Make a Gratitude List of the things you appreciate about yourself from this stage.

_____
_____
_____
_____
_____
_____
_____

What new beliefs might you integrate into your mind from this list?

_____
_____
_____
_____
_____
_____
_____
_____

What new behaviors might you embrace with this conscious awareness?

_____
_____
_____
_____
_____
_____
_____

About the Author

Satya Winkelman, M.A., Psychotherapist, Board Certified in Psychodrama and Group Psychotherapy, is a certified Holistic Health Educator and has studied Art Therapy. She has been a Communication Trainer and Creativity Consultant for Fortune 500 companies in the U.S., Canada and Europe for over 25 years. She was Program Director at Kripalu Holistic Health Center, Lenox, MA, and was Staff Trainer and Director of Psychodrama at Palms Hospital in Sarasota, Florida. Satya continues to facilitate women's empowerment groups working to foster self-awareness, personal and spiritual growth. She has two grown sons, and is a Ceramic Artist. Satya can be contacted at ***www.GuideToTransformation.com***

www.ingramcontent.com/pod-product-compliance
Lightning Source LLC
Chambersburg PA
CBHW041550220426
43666CB00002B/24